A.I.
Cancer
Timebomb

Beware! Be-Aware,
A.I. Bringing Nuclear To Your Town

A.I.
Cancer
Timebomb

A treatise: Warning of the Dangers of Nuclear Radiation. Based on facts with descriptions of:

AI, Past, Present and Future

Nuclear Radiation Basics

Mitochondria Dysfunction and Cancer

Among all the toxins which are carcinogens, the highly dangerous and invisible one, ionizing radiation, is described herein. The connection with AI is due to several AI companies planning to open nuclear plants. Nuclear reactors would provide energy for their computational facilities. However, these plants might also discharge ionizing radiation, as well as nuclear particles into the environment. *The smallest amount of ionizing radiation should be respected.* Numerous examples are described to illustrate current concepts in AI as well as the dangerous causing cancer effects of ionizing radiation. Examples are designed to provide information pertinent to various chapters of the text. All examples conclude with the symbol, #. About fifty references are identified, for further reading and verification.

Charles R Giardina

TABLE OF CONTENTS

Preface

A rigorous account of AI both in the past and more importantly, in the present and future are provided herein. Timely AI descriptions are illustrated for Large Language Models and Natural Language Processing. These are described in terms of the Attention models which underlines Generative Pre-trained Transformer, GPT as well as Chat GPT. All these models employ parallel algorithms. Because of this, data retrieval algorithms, neural network algorithms, data mining as well as transmission operations are shared among many processors. Essentially, all processors can operate in parallel and in a timely fashion. A consequence is that a great deal of energy is needed to power these processors. Moreover, large buildings containing various processors must be moderated. This ensures that no excessive heat exists within the processors.

Several companies running these data centers recently announced their intention to use nuclear reactors to ensure enough power exists to drive their AI operations. Some of these companies, are Google, and Microsoft. Unbelievably, the latter company wants to reopen Three Mile Island. This is the beginning of the AI Cancer Timebomb. *One must respect even the slightest amount of ionizing radiation.* This type of nuclear radiation is a result of fission or fusion. A rigorous description of both, fission and the fusion process is provided within the text proper. Modern day nuclear reactors employ the former process, while proposed future reactors might be of the latter type.

The following chapters describe the types of ionizing radiation emitted from these reactors. Various units are employed for determining the amount of radiation registered directly from the radioactive source. Additionally, units are given specifying amounts of ionizing radiation existing in ambient environments as well as for radiation deposited on human tissue. Even a slight increase in ionizing radiation in the environment should be a scare. It could make an exposed cell become cancerous and forget how to die. The cell could multiply forming a tumor. Worse yet, the cancerous cell could enter the blood stream and spread.

Most importantly and timely, the cause of cancer from ionizing radiation are defects within the mitochondria and damage to its DNA. Descriptions are provided of the DNA within the mitochondria, mtDNA. This type of DNA is more prevalent than the DNA within the nucleus of a cell. There is an average of two thousand mitochondria within a cell, each having one to ten strands of mtDNA. Moreover, the mtDNA are spread out, without having the protection found in nuclear DNA. In particular, there are no histones to protect mtDNA. In fact, each mtDNA forms an exposed circular ring. Background material for DNA are explained, along with descriptions of methylation and histone modification

1) Introduction

1.1) Disciplines Within AI

Artificial Intelligence, AI has existed for years. The subject consists of a combination of concepts derived from engineering and computer science. AI always involves computers or microprocessors, which employ code to demonstrate human type intelligence. Overall, AI can be viewed as two major and almost disjointed disciplines. The first discipline is grounded in the basics of closed loop control systems and mathematical logic. AI, when viewed as a closed loop control system, incorporates robotic technology. In this case, computers and microprocessors act as a brain making decisions. These decisions are arrived at as a consequence of inputs provided by sensors, such as pressure sensors, imaging devices, as well as sonar and the like. Based on these types of inputs, control surfaces are employed. Among the control surfaces are mechanical arms, synthesized voice commands similar to responses from a cell phone, printed text message outputs and so on. The use of various mathematical logic algorithms are programmed into the processors. For instance, a hyper-theoretical command might be: IF the image sensor visualizes a person less than ten feet away THEN do not move. These concepts are described in more depth in Appendix 1.1.

1.2) Large Language Models and Generative AI

The second AI area is more in line with the theme of this text: The AI Cancer Timebomb. This AI discipline is based on Large Language Models, LLM as well as open loop control systems and parallel processing. LLM can be perceived to be a robotic aid, like a smart kiosk or a chatbot. In short, it is an open loop robotic aid which performs Natural Language Processing, NLP in real time. The aid provides answers and responses to human questions, and commands. It replies to queries and demands, as well as having reasoning ability and having common sense capability. These machines often learn how to produce outputs specific to users input questions. The aids often extrapolate and suggest other information associated with the users inputs. These concepts are often referred to as generative AI. Here, neural nets are pre-trained in specific areas of epistemology. This ensures realistic human interactions and expectations. Results are given in various areas and, of most importance, they are given in real time.

Early on, NLP questions and queries were inputted by way of written or typed commands. Later on, smarter aids were constructed allowing inputs of voice commands as well as image and video. The output of these devices could be printed or synthesized voice, images or videos. They could also be original recordings or reports all obtained in a timely fashion. That is, responses are provided in real time. This is the keyer, real time response. Applications vary, from translation from one language into another, also providing medical advice as to the nature of sickness and discomfit. Additionally, they can provide information on protein folding and producing images from worded descriptions. The parallel aspect refers to a simultaneous search for the best and most correct output. This is performed by interrogating several large pre-trained data bases of information, and filtering the gathered information.

Mathematical details of LLM, and parallel processing concepts are presented in greater detail in Chapter 2 as well as in Appendices A1.2, and A2. Because of these models in AI, gigantic buildings were constructed to house multitudes of computers and processors, all operating in parallel. These large buildings are mainly data centers containing processors with knowledge mined from numerous disciplines. Additionally, dedicated processors exist to retrieve, and transmit this knowledge. The results are intelligent systems, such as ChatGPT. GPT stands for Generative Pre-trained Transformers.

Pre-trained means that the neural net aid was previously trained on a large amount of data. The neural net aid already knows the meaning of each word. but for some words there are choices. These words have several distinct meanings. However, the context of all words are determined from the user's total input word sequence. A transformer refers to algorithmic techniques which allow the robotic aid to create meaningful outputs using contextual methods in parallel. Most importantly, results are always provided in real time. Specific domain applications occur in almost every area such as, Farmer GPT, Medical Doctor GPT, Weather GPT, Accountant GPT, Baseball GPT, Coin Collecting GPT etc.

Basics of these types of systems are provided in Chapter 2, along with a description of AI data farms. The latter concept is a term referring to huge buildings containing large numbers of computers working in unison. The more information acquired, the better the robotic aid, since it becomes smarter.

Filtering algorithms are employed to ensure reliable data storage and retrieval.

1.3) Nuclear Energy and Cancer

The gigantic AI data centers need a tremendous amount of electricity to work. Many of the operators of these AI data farms purchased or designated nuclear reactors to power their centers. Some of these plants originally were destined for closure or re-fabrication. The principle purpose of this use of nuclear is for generating energy to support computation and transmission of knowledge. This provides the connection between AI and cancer since nuclear energy is NOT green energy. It could, did, and will cause cancer. This is the core meaning of the AI CANCER TIMEBOMB.

Chapter 3 begins with a many-sorted algebra type of explanation of the fission and fusion processes. Concurrently, numerous examples are provided. These processes are the foundation of nuclear bombs, as well as nuclear reactors. This is followed by a description of both the fission and fusion process from a physics point of view. Nuclear reactors for the purpose of energy generation are illustrated along with the current nuclear situation. In this chapter, descriptions are given of proposed, supposedly less dangerous, and near term

nuclear reactors. Near term refers to about ten years from now. Finally, even safer nuclear fusion reactors are proposed for use some fifty years from now.

Chapter 4 is dedicated in showing the types of radiation emitted from nuclear fission. This is the basic method for energy generation in present day nuclear reactors. Also shown are the consequences of radiated components, as well as measuring the effects of ionizing radiation. Various units are described in ascertaining the amount of ionizing radiation both from the source as well as on exposed body tissue. The latter human acquired radiation is illustrated both qualitatively and quantitatively.

Appendix 3 provides a survey of nuclear involvement mainly for the US throughout the years. In this appendix, numerous deaths and several types of cancers are illustrated that arise due to nuclear involvement. A description of DNA and epigenetic implications are given in Chapter 5. Mutation of DNA due to ionized radiation leading to cancer is also outlined in this chapter. Probably, of more importance is the disorder within the mitochondria and their internal DNA due to ionized radiation. In particular, epigenetic consequences of ionizing radiation are linked to outcomes in cancer. This chapter ends on a happier note - potential remission of cancer.

2) Generative Pre-trained Transformer

2.1) Natural Language Models

In the past, several types of neural networks have been employed for NLP purposes. They all execute in a sequential manner. A brief description of these processors can be found in (Giardina, 2024). They are classified as different types of Recurrent Neural Nets, RNN. They require an ordered processing of data in sequential stages. In this reference, there exists an in-depth mathematical description of basic facts concerning Neural Networks, NN, and how they 'learn'. Also, discussed is the LSTM, which is the Long Short Term Memory, NN. This type of NN is an improvement over the RNN, but still it must operate in a sequential manner. See (Sutskever, et al, 2014), for a more in-depth treatment of LSTM. As mentioned previously, the LSTM is a sequential processing unit, however, it uses an encoder/ decoder mechanism. This device first employs the encoder to convert words into a numerical type quantity. In turn, among other things, the decoder provides words corresponding to these assigned numerical quantities.

In 2017 the transformer model for NLP was described by (Vaswani,et al, 2017). This paper, again uses an encoder/decoder mechanism. It opened the doors to numerous applications involving LLM. A detailed diagram of the transformer model is provided in Figure 2.1 below. The major benefit of this model is that transformers involve parallel algorithms. Parallel information implementation enable many processors to operate on a gigantic amount of data, all at the same time. Parallelism and simultaneity ensures that NLP occurs in real time. Here, numerous processes each share distinct parts of the overall algorithm. When finished, another processor can collect the results and perform filtering. Additionally, the training time for neural networks is also lessoned as compared to sequential models.

Language consists of an ordered countable string of words, and in RNN they had to be processed sequentially. In the transformer protocol each word or sub-word is mapped into a quantity called a token. Tokens within the input string are mapped into unique real numbers. A distinct token is provided for a period as the indication for the end of a sentence.

Additionally, the symbol ’ s ‘ is often utilized to denote the start of a sentence. Assigning unique numerical values for every toke enable tokens to not get lost. They can be located without searching, even if the original order is disturbed. This is crucial when distinct tokens are extracted and compared to each other and then processed in parallel.

Other novel protocols involving the transformer model are the attention mechanisms. These mechanisms not only allow long sequences of input words to occur, but also take into account the context. To begin, self attention is a method for providing weights indicating the relationship between every token with every other token including itself, all within the input string. Numerous relation operators can be employed, again in a parallel manner. The relation could be statistical, for instance, using the probability that a word in English ends with ‘ing’. It could involve morphological structures or coincidences, such as that the phrase ‘ it is’ appears within a certain context. More importantly, tokens early in the input string can be compared semantically to tokens that are much further down the string. The consequence of this long reference window is illustrated in the example below.

Example 2.1)

Say that the word ‘neuron’ exists early in an input sentence. Then later, within the input string, a mention of ‘neural network’ is specified. It would then be known that the semantic context ensures that the ‘neuron’ would be a node within a ‘neural network’. This observation by the transformer model is due to the Pre-training aspect in GPT. Pre-training associates the word ‘neuron’ with nodes, or computational units within a neural network.

Within a neuron, a computation is performed. It is called an affine transformation. This transformation is just several multiplications and an addition computation. Similar operations are performed within every node of the neural network structures. However, on the other hand, suppose that later on in the input sequence, the mention of a ‘cell’ is given instead of a ‘neural network’. Then it would be known that the ‘neuron’ would refer instead to a part of a human’s brain. Again, from the context of the long sentence different meanings of a single word are identified.#

2.2) Transformer Description

Transformers generate text, one word or token at a time. A token is usually a whole word, but it could instead represent part of a word. For instance, there may be two tokens for the word 'can't' - they are, ' can ', and ' ' t '. Additionally, there are tokens to start and stop a sentence, the period is a token '.' . The transformers are used to answer questions, to play music or songs, to provide pictures of objects and even to translate input from one language into another. Whatever the application, there are a tremendous amount of computations to be performed. However, the computations are shared using numerous processors and this is due to the parallelism which exists within the algorithms. In general, the transformer model predicts the next word in a sentence. Each of the numerous components within the transformer model are provided in Figure 2.1. The transformer will be described in the context of translating an input string, from one language into another. This is performed one token at a time.

The overall process begins as the input string enters the encoder. The output of the encoder is a string of vectors corresponding to the inputs. Subsequently, they are fed into the decoder as one of the three inputs of the multi head attention block. See Figure

2.1. Here, the information calculated, which is the output of the encoder, is applied to the decoder in the center of this device. In this translation application the output token from the decoder is fed back into the decoder's bottom input section. This occurs until an end of sentence token is generated. When the sentence end token appears the transformer begins again afresh as an initial condition. It then uses the first token after the end token occurred. The process goes on until the end of all input tokens occur.

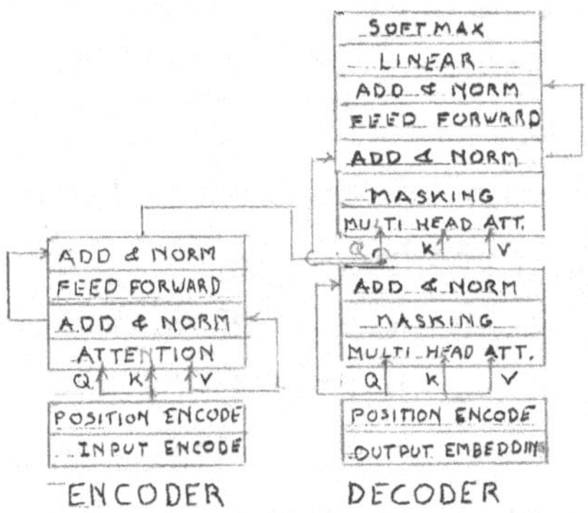

FIGURE 2.1) Transformer Architecture

To illustrate the overwhelming computational burden of this model, specifics are provided next for each sub block within the input process. It begins in the encoder block. The first input sub block is input encode, more often called input embedding. This block translates each token into a vector of real numbers which represent the specific token. The output, or result from this first block, is called the input embedding vector.

The elements within each vector are found using neural networks. Elements within the vectors are also called tuples. These values associate certain characteristics of the token and map them into real numbers. The vectors can be considered to occur by using a look - up table. Very simple examples follow. They are given for motivation, as well as describing technical concepts relative to the goals of the text: These objectives are: Providing a tutorial on AI old and new; Describing nuclear power; Illustrating the effects of ionizing radiation on human tissue; And providing the latest information of methods for cancer remission.

Example 2.2)

Refer to Example 2.1. As before, suppose that the context involving the input sequence is that the token 'neuron' is referring to neural networks. Also, assume that this token has an embedding representation involving the row vector consisting of two tuples (3.4 .2). A different token associated with neural networks will have an embedding vector with tuples close to those of the neuron. Closeness intuitively means that numerical values of elements in the same tuple positions are close. Actually, an inner product is employed, and for those interested, this is explained and illustrated in Appendix A2..2.

Suppose that, within the input string, a word appears which is used very often in describing neural networks. Specifically, say that 'activation', appears. In this case, the corresponding token for this word might have an embedding vector, (3.2 .4). Note that the entries within this vector are similar in size with those for a 'neuron'. Tokens having nothing to do with neural networks, have embedding vectors with tuples far from those of 'neuron'.

The word 'activation' was employed since most nodes of a neural network also contain an activation function. This function is applied after the affine transformation and is usually a non linear function.#

An additional example is provided next. It again is simplified, but it provides supplemental information useful in the following chapters. More details in the embedding process can be found in Appendix A2.1.

Example 2.3)

Again refer to Example 2.1, but this time assume that the word 'neuron' refers to a part of a human's brain. If this is known, then the word embedding mechanism in the transformer would again realize that other words involving the brain should have corresponding vectors close to that of 'neuron'. Using the Pre-training aspect within GPT, an initial embedding is performed. For this situation, assume the embedding vector for 'neuron' is (9 5.1). Note that this embedded vector is different from the one used in Example 2.2. This occurred because a different context was observed by the neural networks during pre-training. The new context was remembered by the embedding device.

Each of the one hundred billion neurons within the brain would have a corresponding embedding vector (9 5.1). Suppose that the input sentence also contained the word 'mitochondria'. These are the energy producing sub cells or organelles within the neuron. Each neuron contains up to two thousand of these mitochondria. Then the word 'mitochondria', when observed in the input string, would have an initial embedding close to that of 'neuron'. For instance, the embedding vector might be (8 4.9).#

In the primary reference, (Vaswani, et al, 2017), it is mentioned that each token within the input string is word embedded into a 512 tuple vector of real numbers. Not just two tuples, as illustrated in the previous examples. However, again words with similar context are close. Words with little semantic connection have vector representations with tuples appearing farther apart. The previous examples illustrated the concept of homographs. These are words with the same spelling, but have distinct conceptual meanings. Appendix A2.1 explains this concept in greater detail and compares it to the more popular notion of homonyms.

The next block within the input assembly assigns a vector to each token within the input stream. It indicates the order of occurrence for the token involved. This concept was briefly mentioned before. The vector is called the position encoding vector and it is added to the input embedding vector. More in depth details on the position recording procedure are described, along with examples, in Appendix A2.2. The resulting vector is called the summed vector.

The summed vectors are then inputted simultaneously into both the multi headed attention block and also into the add norm block. Within the multi headed attention block, self attention is applied.

This concept was conceptually described in Section 2.1. Again, it associates every word with every other word within the input sequence. This is the most important step in the whole process. The next example reinforces the self attention mechanism.

Example 2.4)

Consider the long sentence with tokens equal to whole words being inputted into the transformer: 'When nuclear reactors generate energy to power AI data farms, the radiation emitted increases chances of mitochondria disfunction and can cause cancer.' If attention is given to pairs of words within this sentence and their context, a result is that it is easily seen that certain words can be grouped together. For instance, the words 'nuclear', and 'radiation', can be grouped together. Similarly, the words 'mitochondria' and 'cancer' form another grouping.

However, other words within this input seemingly do not have similar contextual connection, for instance, 'nuclear', and 'farms' have little correlation. By keeping track of every word within the input, the attention mechanism assigns numerical values to every pair of tokens. Those that have similar groupings are assigned numerical values which are close. On the other hand, words not having similar context have numerical values farther apart.#

The actual steps in producing self attention involve the query, key and value matrices. These matrices are found before the attention process begins. Ultimately, by use of these matrices a scoring matrix is acquired. It illustrates the strength of the association of every token to all other tokens within the input string. Subsequently, scaling is performed, and then a softmax operation is carried out. The latter operation provides probability values associated with each input token pair. The larger the probability corresponds to pairs of tokens more highly contextually connected. Additional mathematical details are provided in Appendix 2.3.

In the decoder, algorithms are almost identical to those in the encoder stage. A large exception is that the decoder cannot predict, that is, it cannot utilize tokens later specified within the input string. In short, causality must be conducted. It makes certain that the prediction of the next word only depends upon the present and previous words, and not future words.

2.3) AI Data Farms

AI data farms consist of very large buildings containing a tremendously large number of computers and processors. A substantial amount of energy is needed for powering these devices. Energy is also consumed for moderating the temperature within the buildings that house these processing units. Some AI data centers are used primarily for neural net training. Other data centers are dedicated to deploying the information in real time to users. The connection with cancer is that the energy source to operate these data centers is by and large nuclear. Nuclear Energy is NOT Green Energy. A forever lasting invisible danger exists due to ionizing radiation.

The data centers have ranks based on scores involving their availability, reliability, and redundancy. There exists four tiers used in classifying the goodness of these data centers:

Tier 1) Little redundancy, 28.8 hours down time per year

Tier 2) Some redundancy, 22 hours down time per year

Tier 3) Numerous power sources and cooling paths, on line maintenance 1.6 hours down time per year

Tier 4) Redundancy at the component level leading to full fault tolerance, 26.3 minutes down time per year. (Sayegh, 2024).

It would appear that centers with higher tier numbers would require more energy than lower tiered ones. Since 2020, average power per rack of AI processors went from eight thousand watts, that is 8 kW, to 17 kW. By 2027, the expectation is 30 kW. ChatGPT consumes 80 kW per rack, and Nvidia's new AI chip needs 120 kW per rack. AI is expected to increase data center power demand by the amount of 160% by 2030. Typical racks are 32 inches wide, by 48 inches deep, by 90 inches high, and are loaded with computers and processors.

Use of Chat GPT when asking a question is less energy efficient than a usual computer search. The former uses 10 to 25 times more energy than standard computer searches. About ten million questions are asked of ChatGPT per day. The energy used for obtaining replies could power about two million homes. In a single hour, Google's AI uses enough energy to power 25,000 electric cars. It is said that generative AI will use ten times more energy by 2026 than it did in 2023. (Scientific American, 2025). AI farms are expected to use 1000 tera-watt hours by 2026. By 2030 energy could be 50 times higher than today. Energy needed to power AI server farms and data base centers double every 100 days. Use of nuclear to generate this energy is a time bomb.

3) Nuclear Energy

3.1) Fission and Fusion Processes, A Mathematical Perspective

The history of nuclear energy is described in Appendix 3, involving fission and fusion. In the following, these two types of nuclear energy are described and illustrated in a many-sorted polyadic type diagram, provided in Figure 3.1. This diagram provides a high view of the fission and fusion process. For a succinct description of polyadic diagrams see (Giardina, 2025). In the fission and fusion process, the polyadic graph is modified somewhat from the reference above. Here, the polyadic arrow can have several arrow pointers, that is, several arrow heads, as well as the traditional many tailed arrows. Additionally, a dotted arrow illustrates that zero or one or two…, of the sort result from the operation named above the arrow. The operator name associated with this many tailed, many pointed arrow can be identified as a vector valued function. However, in the following it will be referred to as a relation.

Figure 3.1A, illustrates the process of nuclear fission. The left circle is a node; within the circle the sort ATOM is identified. This sort refers to whole atoms provided in the Periodic Table of Elements, abbreviated, PTE. Sort ATOM also includes these atoms as well as their isotopes. Isotopes are elements with the same number of protons, but with more, equal or less neutrons as elements described within this table. Atoms and their isotopes have the same atomic number. The right circle within Figure 3.1A, has sort NEUTRON, referring to neutrons within some atom or some isotope. Neutrons have mass one just like protons, but with no charge. The bottom circle in this diagram indicates sort FRAGMENT. The latter sort refers to parts of an atom, rarely the whole atom. Additionally, FRAGMENT also includes energy emitted by nuclear reactions. These are alpha particles, beta particles, gamma rays as well as electro magnetic radiation described in Section 4.3.

In Figure 3.1A, the arrow with two tails and two solid arrows and a dotted arrow is labeled FISSION. It is a relation illustrating that when sort ATOM and sort NEUTRON are employed the results are two sorts of ATOM, and a zero, or one, or two, or three... sort of FRAGMENT. In the examples provided below the plus sign '+' to the left means collides with. The arrow, ' —-> ' means becomes. The plus sign to the right of the arrow means also.

Example 3.1)

Suppose that a singe neutron bombards Uranium 235, which has atomic number 92, that is it has 92 protons. Its atomic weight is 235, this is the combined number of neutrons plus protons. It is denoted by ${}^{235}_{92}U$. When the FISSION process occurs various fission fragments can arise such as Barium and Krypton, specifically:

$${}^{235}_{92}U + {}^{1}_{0}n \text{ —-> } {}^{141}_{56}Ba + {}^{92}_{36}Kr + 3\,{}^{1}_{0}n.$$

The equation above illustrates this fission process. Here, a neutron having mass one, and zero charge, denoted by ${}^{1}_{0}n$ hits, or collides with the uranium isotope. It results in two sorts of ATOM, namely Barium and Krypton, along with three sorts of FRAGMENT, all being the same. In this case, the particle is a neutron.#

In Figure 3.1B, a polyadic type graph illustrates the fusion process. In the diagram there are two sorts; in the upper node sort ATOM is designated, as in the fission process. On the bottom is a node indicating sort FRAGMENT. The relation this time is indicated using the two tailed, two arrowed FUSION operation. Thus when two sorts of ATOM are employed the result is a single sort ATOM along with zero, one, two, ... sort of FRAGMENT. Since the dotted arrow points to FRAGMENT. The next example illustrates the fusion process. It involves two isotopes of hydrogen not located in the PTE. The atom with atomic number one is within the PTE. It is the first element within this table and has no neutrons. It is denoted by ${}^{1}_{0}H$, and it has one proton and one electron. The atomic mass is one, because the electron has almost zero mass.

A different isotope of hydrogen is used in the fusion process besides ${}^{1}_{0}H$. It is described below, and is called a deuterium isotope ${}^{2}_{0}H$. It is often denoted by D, and is part of a heavy water molecule, D_2O. Deuterium has exactly one of each, neutron, proton, and electron. Additionally, its atomic mass is two, and its charge is zero. It collides with a tritium isotope ${}^{3}_{0}H$. This isotope has a single proton and electron, but has two neutrons. The atomic weight in this case is three.

Example 3.2)

When deuterium collides with tritium they produce a helium atom, $^{4}_{0}He$ along with a neutron. Additionally, some release of kinetic energy, ke, is radiated. The energy accounts for the total mass to the left of the arrow, being greater than the sum of the masses to the right of the arrow. In short:

$$^{2}_{0}H + ^{3}_{0}H \dashrightarrow ^{4}_{0}He + ^{1}_{0}n + ke.$$

The fusion process results in a helium atom along with a single neutron. Additionally, kinetic energy is released .#

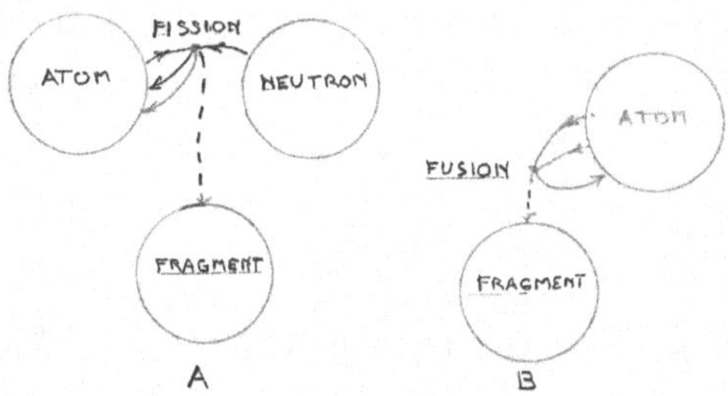

FIGURE 3.1) Polyadic Graphs for Fission and Fusion

In short, the fission process refers to the process of splitting an entity into two entities, and fusion refers to the combining of two entities into a single one. These concepts are mentioned here because the mitochondria has the ability to do both of these actions. See Section 5.4. The mitochondria is the energy source for cells within the body. It's DNA; mtDNA is very susceptible to ionizing radiation, and enforces the theme of this text: The AI CANCER TIMEBOMB. Finally, it should be mentioned that quantum tunneling exists in both the fission and fusion processes. For a description of quantum tunneling see, (Giardina, 2024). In nuclear fission, some radioactive particles of the alpha type, tunnel through potential energy barriers involving the nucleus of an isotope. Additionally, all types of fusion involving the mitochondria usually involve quantum tunneling. An interesting related paper is, (Vincent, et al, 2017).

3.2) Splitting Of An Atom In A Nuclear Reactor

The employment of nuclear reactors has similarities with the usage of nuclear bombs. They both involve heavy atoms, usually uranium 235, sometimes plutonium 239, and rarely other heavy atoms. These atoms contain a large number of protons, as well as neutrons. When many molecules of these atoms are contained in a densely populated region, and a neutron hits this configuration, it splits into several parts. The parts include smaller atomic numbered isotopes. The process is described in the previous section as nuclear fission. This result is mainly due to the strong repulsive forces of positive charges oscillating and vibrating within the nucleus. The force of the neutron hitting the isotope overrides the nuclear attractions holding the nucleus together. The consequence of this collision produces a substance called fission products. These products consist of two or three atoms or isotopes, all of a lower atomic number. Additionally, a number of stray neutrons are formed, and possibly other forms of energy. When a critical mass exists, the stray neutrons hit different heavy atoms and new fission products are a result. The process can continue indefinitely, unless it explodes as a bomb, or the process is slowed down and ultimately ceases.

In the above it is assumed that a super critical fission occurs. This means that there is enough nuclear material densely packed in an enclosure to sustain the continued fission process. In this case, the isotopes are called a critical mass. Additionally, reflectors are often employed in a nuclear reactor at the boundaries of a container holding the nuclear material. Reflectors improve the probability of neutron material colliding with isotopes, thus enhancing the fission process. Reflecting material is also called tamper. Sometimes tamper involves a liquid such as water. For nuclear reactors, a cylinder type of containment is often employed. See Figure 3.2. In a nuclear reactor, control rods are entered into the cylinder, thereby controlling the speed of the fission process. These rods absorb neutrons and therefore slow down the reaction. The more they are inserted into the reactor, the slower the fission process occurs, until it stops or explodes. For a bomb a small hollow spherical configuration is often used. An isotope of tritium is often employed within the interior, thus causing a fusion process. There are no control rods in this case.

The specific type of nuclear reactor portrayed in the below figure is classified as a BWR, Boiling Water Reactor. This is a reactor in which the same water cooling the nuclear material drives the turbine. In this case, the water is called the core water. Most of the time, the material used within the reactor is uranium which heats the core water, and subsequent steam drives the turbine. It is often called a single line water reactor. However, the condenser illustrated in the figure has a separate line for the cooling water. Using heat transfer, the cooling water enables the temperature of core water to be lessened. This design was attributed to Admiral Hyman Rickover, and the reactor was built by GE. See Appendix 3 for a more in-depth nuclear involvement with GE, as well as the Pressurized Water Reactors, PWR. The latter types of reactors are more prevalent in the US and were mainly built by Westinghouse. In this situation, a separate water line produces steam to drive the turbine. Additionally in this case, the condenser uses heat from the core water to heat the secondary water stream by heat transfer. The secondary water stream produce steam to generate the turbine.

Example 3.3)

Consider, ${}^{235}_{92}U$, recall, this is the symbol for for uranium whose atomic number is 92, and whose mass is 235. When a single neutron, symbolized by ${}^{1}_{0}n$, hits the uranium particle, new particles can be created similar to the ones illustrated in Example 3.1. The nucleus of uranium splits into two or more smaller nuclei as well as other particles. For instance, single particles of Rhodium, Rh, with atomic number 45 are created. Additionally, isotopes of Silver, Ag with atomic number 47, are produced.

Furthermore, three neutrons are formed. The three neutrons are denoted by 3 $^{1}_{0}$n, where each neutron has mass one and charge zero. These new neutrons each create new fission particles. This occurs by a neutron hitting another $^{235}_{92}$U, isotope.

The associated masses of each resulting single particle are, 115, 118, and 1 respectively. This fission process is mathematically described as:

$$^{235}_{92}U + ^{1}_{0}n \longrightarrow ^{115}_{45}Rh + ^{118}_{47}Ag + 3\,^{1}_{0}n$$

Conservation of mass and energy are illustrated in this equation. Specifically on the left side of this equation, the total mass is 235 + 1 = 236. On the right hand side of this equation, 115 + 118 + 3 (1) = 236. Similarly, the net charge on both sides is 92.#

Additional illustrations of nuclear fission involving large neutron to proton ratios is illustrated below. Again uranium is involved yielding fragments which are extremely radioactive.

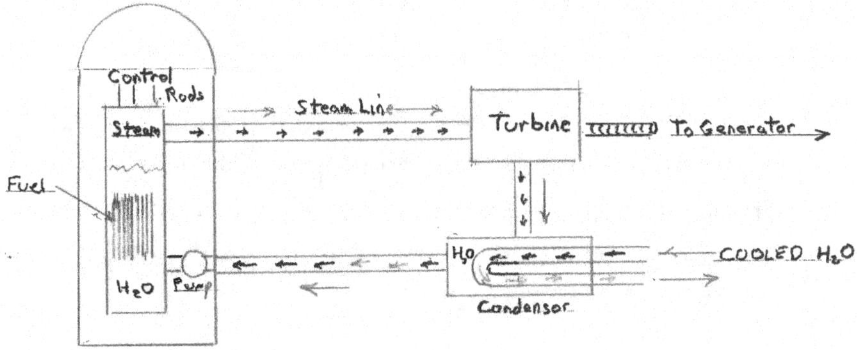

FIGURE 3.2) Basics of a Nuclear Reactor

Example 3.4)

Suppose that a single neutron bombards ${}^{235}_{92}U$, just like in Example 3.3. Various fission fragments can arise, these include, Iridium and Yttrium. The mathematical equation describing the fission process is:

$$ {}^{235}_{92}U + {}^{1}_{0}n \longrightarrow {}^{131}_{53}I + {}^{89}_{39}]Y + 16\,{}^{1}_{0}n. $$

Several other byproducts of nuclear fission involving Uranium can occur.#

Examples 3.3 and 3.4 illustrate binary fission products since two distinct isotopes arise, along with several neutrons. There are times in which three distinct isotopes can occur, and this is called trinary fission products. In the latter case the same polyadic diagram as in Figure 3.1, can represent this process. This illustrates the rare case, where FRAGMENT can refer to a whole atom or isotope, and not just a component of an isotope.

3.3) Creation of Nuclear Material

Highly Enriched Uranium, HEU is at least twenty percent of Uranium 235, and the rest being Uranium 238. It is formed by way of an enrichment process. The 235 isotope exists in nature; it can be found as a very small percentage integrated within natural mined Uranium 238. Quantitatively, U235 molecules are found at a .7 percentage among molecules of U238. After mining, a milling process follows and finally the enrichment stage, or stages, are performed. The U235 isotope, being lighter than the U238 isotope, is usually separated by a centrifuge enrichment forcing device. As in any centrifugal force, the heavier isotopes go to the farthest distance from the Darboux vector. This vector represents the center axis performing the angular velocity. Simultaneously, the somewhat lighter HEU stays close to the axis of rotation due to the centripetal force. These molecules are what is needed.

Accordingly, these particles are extracted. These extracted particles might go through another additional centrifuge enrichment process,.

Low Enriched Uranium LEU, usually has more than .7 percent, but less than 10 percent, of U235. Depleted Uranium consists of less than .7 percent of U235. For weapons grade Uranium, about 90% of U235 is often desired. Usually, there are numerous centrifuges cascaded together providing higher and higher HEU in later stages, as mentioned above.

Plutonium is also both used in weapons and in nuclear reactors. In particular, the isotope Pu239 is employed. It is not found naturally; it must be created before it can be used. For reactor applications, Pu239 is usually 70% pure while for weapons grade applications 90% purity is desired. This substance has a higher neutron emission, and higher radiation as well as higher temperature tolerance than U238, in all applications. However, Plutonium 239 is formed after mining, and milling U238, then using a nuclear reaction. Illustrated in Example 3.5 below.

Bombardment by neutrons causes some resulting Uranium to absorb neutrons. This spent fuel is then separated into U238 isotopes as well as all the other fission products. In this case, reprocessing is performed chemically. For conventional electricity generation from a nuclear reactor, Pu239 is used just like U235.

Example 3.5)

When U238 molecules are bombarded by neutrons, they become very unstable U239 molecules, with a loss of electrons. A single atom loses a single electron, and the overall charge for the atom becomes positive.#

There are several fissile nuclear fuels. These are the materials which can undergo nuclear fission when struck by a low energy neutron. The main four are U235, Pu239, U233, and U232. The first only exists mixed with U238 at a percentage of .7%. The others are man made in nuclear reactors, as illustrated in the above example. The molecules of Pu239 are created from U238 at a percentage of 3% as a by product of this Uranium. Molecules of U233 are created from Thorium 232, which is not fissile. Again, a nuclear reactor is employed. Thorium 232 is further described in Section 3.5. The Thorium fission process takes an average of thirty days to create U233. A byproduct of U233 is U232, which is an obstacle for the use of U233 in a nuclear reactor. It has a half life of almost 70 years, and must be handled using remote techniques within shielded containment centers. On the other hand, it is less desirable for weapon use than U235. (Lloyd, et al, 2019).

Besides the PWR by Westinghouse, and the BWR by GE, another similar water cooled reactor is CANDU, CANanada's DeUterium reactor. This reactor was first built in the 1960s for use in Canada. It differs from the light water reactors just mentioned, since it involves heavy water, D_2O. However, a beneficial feature is that it can produce fission from only U238. Additionally, since the radioactive fuel consists of numerous uranium rods, when the radioactivity is low within a rod it can be replaced. This ensures that the reactor can be refueled on line. It need not be shut down for refueling.

3.4) The Current State of Nuclear and Some of Their Problems

Currently there are 440 nuclear power plants in the world. Sixty exist in the US. Under President Trump's first administration several nuclear plants were destined to be closed.

In March 2024, Amazon purchased a 100% nuclear powered data center for 650 million dollars. The nuclear plant is the sixth largest in the US. It is a 960 megawatt facility, and is located outside Berwick Penn. (electrak, 2024). As of June 2024, Bill Gates is building a nuclear powered plant for AI purposes in Wyoming,. It is called Natrium, and is a molten salt reactor. Liquid Sodium is the coolant, and it is a fast reactor. The use of appropriate containment equipment enables real time refueling. Additionally, there is a heat transfer unit to exchange the heat from the the coolant to water containment. The heated water produces steam to turn the turbines, thus producing energy in a standard fashion.

In Sept 2024 Microsoft purchased Three Mile Island nuclear plant in Penn. (NPC news, 2024). Three Mile Island nuclear plant will reopen to power Microsoft data centers in about four years, (NPC news, 2024). Google purchased, in July 2024, a nuclear reactor in Tennessee, evidencing that (BBC, 2024). Google is turning towards nuclear to power its AI data centers, (BBC, 2024). Along the same line, Open AI wants to power AI farms with nuclear power. Open AI is the supplier of all versions of ChatGPT throughout the world.

For sustaining fission, it is important to maintain critical mass. This was mentioned in Section 3.2. Here, refueling of the nuclear reactors must be performed such that there is a high density of nuclear material to support the fission process. Refueling in real time is risky because it makes the AI CANCER TIMEBOMB inevitable.

Among the major problems with nuclear reactors is where to dispose of the nuclear waste. The problem also exists with other so called green energy generators. Landfills, consisting of out of service panels and windmills, also pose a cancer threat due to toxic metals deposited. For instance, in Iowa, South Dakota and Wyoming, these toxins are discarded. Wind turbines utilize radioactive Neodymium, Nd, and Dysprosium, Dy.. About five million pounds of radioactive waste are given off annually from these devices. This is a drop in the bucket, compared to nuclear reactor waste materials. Waste in present reactors contain highly reactive actinides. They waste about 99% of fuel which is utilized in the fission process. Through the fission, process U238 converts to non used Neptunium, Np. Subsequently, it becomes Lawrencium, Lr. This isotope has a half life of tens of thousands of years. There is no place safe on earth to store this substance. Deposit locations for ionized particles must be earthquake free, tsunami free, and safe from terrorists, etc.

Nuclear waste does not only occur from nuclear reactors used for electricity generation. It also occurs from US essential nuclear fission and fusion applications. These include experimental nuclear research devices, as well as small nuclear reactors to power numerous submarines. Nuclear reactors are also used in powering other ships for the US Navy. These nuclear wastes must also be contained. Additionally, nuclear waste arises from hospitals, and also from defense purposes. With all these essential applications of nuclear, it does not make sense to use nuclear reactors for electricity generation. In particular, there is no need for nuclear energizing AI data farms. These farms are proposed to become ubiquitous. Gas, coal, oil and hydro work fine for powering AI applications. Unlike radiation, toxins from some of these materials do not last forever. Moreover, these toxins can be seen, unlike the invisible threat of nuclear radiation.

The amount of nuclear waste due solely to Uranium as of Dec., 2021, is given in metric tons by states within the US, (NEI, 2022). A metric ton consists of 2,204 pounds, which is about ten percent more than a usual ton. The total amount of nuclear waste in the

US is 88,345 million metric tons. For instance, samples of waste in metric tons from this report are by state: California, 3,455; Florida, 3,691; Idaho, 153; Illinois, 11,156; North Carolina, 4,562; Pennsylvania, 8,140. Interestingly, Idaho is storing nuclear waste from the Three Mile Island disaster. See Appendix A3, for a brief description of the 1979 Three Mile Island disaster.

In his second administration President Trump, is bringing back the expansion of fossil fuel production. Coal and gas are ten times more efficient than wind, and about twenty times more efficient than solar power. Emissions from coal can be seen, those from nuclear cannot. *A consequence is an invisible clear and present danger.* This again is the AI CANCER TIME BOMB.

3.5) Future Plans For Nuclear Plants and More Problems

Ex President Biden signed the Advanced Nuclear Energy Act. He planned to triple US nuclear production by 2050, and asked for billions of dollars for nuclear development. The Senate passed the bill to appropriate these monies and so did Congress.

Twenty other countries also plan to triple nuclear production by the same time. Many reactors that were proposed are considered to be small, some are modular, and a few are portable.

Small Modular Reactors, SMRs are about one tenth the size of traditional nuclear reactors and can produce a third of the energy. They occupy about 65 acres of land as opposed to 3,000 acres, required for traditional nuclear reactors. The coolant is almost always liquid sodium, See Appendix A.3 for more information about this type of coolant. Amazon, Google, and Microsoft propose to place SMRs in close proximity to existing, and numerous prepossessed AI data farms. These companies also want to use SMRs for other types of data centers. In years to come, hundreds and even thousands of SMRs are predicted to be built. Cameco is a major player in nuclear energy. A deep concern for these types of reactors is that their prevalence requires extreme security measures and careful monitoring.

The next step for future SMR is to use Liquid Fluoride Thorium Reactors. LFTRs. Thorium, Th 232, can be used now, provided that the needed reactor exists. Th 232 isotope is a silvery rock like metal, and is three to four times more prevalent than Uranium. However, it costs more to mine. It is a slightly radioactive material and used in light bulbs and cameras. A nuclear reactor using Thorium employs a heat exchange mechanism. It produces steam from heated water. This is performed in a separate pipe with heated steam to turn the turbines and generate electricity. These reactors are small relative to the conventional nuclear reactors and are also referred to as SMRs. Often they can be utilized in a portable manner, and transported on large trucks.

By 2030, very small Thorium reactors are being planned for commercial use. There is very little waste in these reactors, because nearly all the Thorium is utilized in the reaction. This is unlike Uranium reactors which have some ninety percent waste materials. Molten metals or molten salts allow higher temperatures and lower pressures than water. These reactors are also called molten salt reactors, MSR, because the fuel is in liquid form. Purification techniques are employed in the molten material stages to prevent corrosion. Still, there is danger in any nuclear reactor. Faults in components still exist as well as human failure.

A proposed solution is to use fast nuclear reactive which are capable of breeding. A nuclear reactor which produces more nuclear fuel than it uses is said to breed. Fast neutron reactors which employ U238 usually also require twenty percent U235. Thorium TH232, is fertile it is not fissile and so it has to be bred in order to produce fissionable material. This means that very high speed neutrons must collide with this substance in order to produce fission. In this respect, it is different from U238, which is used in thermal reactors. Thermal reactors usually have moderators to slow down the neutrons. Additionally, some type of kick starter fuel is often needed in order to start the initial process. This fuel could be low enriched uranium, it could also be Plutonium-Beryllium, Pu-Be. Upon nuclear collision with U238, absorption occurs and ultimately fissile Plutonium 239, Pu239 is produced. Collision of neutrons with Thorium produces Protactinium 233, Pa233 and then converts to U233. Although not as good for bombs as Pu239, it still can be used in producing wanted or non wanted bombs. Again, an AI CANCER TIMEBOMB.

Benefits of LFTR, Liquid Fluoride Thorium Reactor. Liquids are efficient, it has nuclide economy, since fissile products can be taken out in real time. Refueling is claimed to be performed in this non time wasting manner. Additionally, it is reported that almost 100% of the fuel in the reactor will be used up during the fission process. This is in contrast to 4%

usage in a uranium reactor. Th232 is easy and safe to mine, process and store, however mining is costly. The reactor operates at low pressure, and it is said to be walk away safe. It has a freeze plug, which allows self shut down in case of over heating. There are no fuel cells in smaller reactors. Figure 3.3, illustrates the process of creating Fissionable U233 from Th232. In Figure 3.3A), a neutron hits Th232, creating Th233 when a beta particle hits it. In about thirty minutes, Th233 is converted into Pa233. Then in a few months, Pa233 releases another beta particle and finally transforms into U233.

Figure 3.3B, illustrates the chemical electrolysis process involved in the last transformation. Modest voltage drives metallic Thorium off the electrode into the left containment salt. Similarly, the Pa molecules on the electrode go into fuel salt carrier. Then after the electrolyses, they are extracted and stored for about a

month until it turns into U233. After this process, the substance is refueled into the reactor.

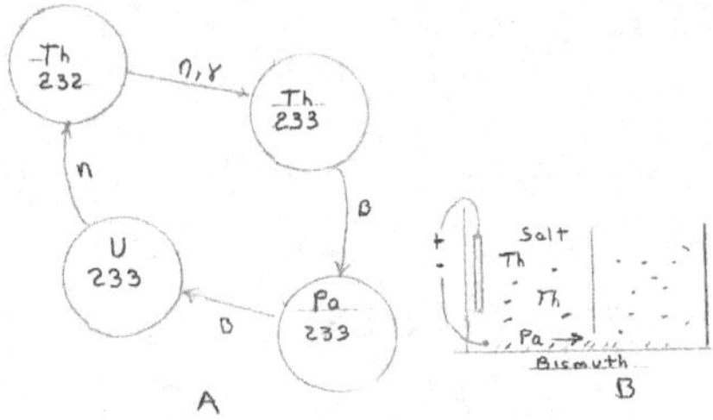

FIGURE 3.3) Thorium to Uranium Cycle

Additional negative aspects of LFTR, follow. Anti corrosion techniques must be performed as a real time maintenance protocol. This is because of the high concentration of salt. Further, a result of the reaction is that U233 is created, and this isotope can be used as a bomb making material. The material can get into the wrong hands, resulting in danger. There is also an eventual creation of U232, which transforms into Th208. The result is an isotope yielding high energy gamma radiation which is very difficult to shield. One should be aware of the slightest amount of additional ionizing radiation.

In 2021 China tested a Thorium nuclear reactor China announced that it will build a 373MW reactor by 2030. India has one third of earth's thorium and has already built a thorium reactor.

Westinghouse proposed advanced safety designs for PWR. These original designs were known to appear in the AP600. It was certified in 1999, and later the AP1000 was proposed with a similar supposedly safe design. These reactors are said to generate 600MWatt, and 1000MWatt energy, respectively. The Obama administration provided loans to Vogtle Electric, in Georgia, to buy two AP1000s. The Obama administration also loaned monies to Virgil Summer Nuclear Center in South Carolina, to buy two AP1000. The two nuclear plants in Georgia were fully completed in 2023 and 2024. However, an overall price of approximately thirty billion dollars was needed as well as a delay of several years. The South Carolina plants were never completed. This resulted in a loss of twenty billion dollars. As a consequence, Westinghouse filed for bankruptcy in 2017. (Patel, 2017). The resulting scandal was labeled Nuke-gate.

Between Obama's purchase of numerous wind power generators and the Fukushima disaster in 2011, The creation of any other nuclear reactors was delayed until 2024. The supposedly second most dangerous nuclear disaster was at Fukushima,. It involved a modified BWR which was built by GE. a diagram of this type of reactor is provided in Figure 3.2.

Small Modular Reactors, SMR are not new. For instance, they have been used in submarines since the 1950's. SMR are classified as reactors generating 300MWatts or less. There are almost a hundred different designs for SMR. Several SMR can be designed at distinct places and then assembled on location. Builders of these reactors all claim that SMRs are safer than water cooled reactors. Because the liquid material can be drained before a SCRAM might occur, the technique is referred to as walk away safety, and was mentioned previously.

The GE company is proposing the GEBRX-300. This nuclear reactor is a BWR version 10, and uses natural water circulation. See Figure 3.2, for a diagram of this type of reactor. However, GE proposed an isolation condenser, which is a tank of water above the reactor. In a SCRAM there is enough water to prevent damage for seven days.

Both Canada and Poland plan to acquire SMR type nuclear reactors within a few years.

4) Radiation

4.1) Types of Radiation

Radiation is usually not harmful. Radiation from a source can move electrons from one orbit to another, or even lose electrons. Radiation occurs from many objects. The stars emit radiation, so does the heat from hot payment. Also microwaves, as well as radio waves, cell phones, and infrared waves all produce radiation. The harmful types of radiation are those that are ionizing. IR denotes Ionizing Radiation, which produces high energy and causes atoms to ionize. Specifically, IR causes electrons to fall off or be added onto an atom. It can cause radiation burns, and the amount of IR absorbed is called the radiation dose. If the whole body is exposed, numerous cells can die, and subsequently cause organs to fail. This happens even in UV radiation from the sun. It can cause DNA to change its code, forming mutations or breaking the code. Specifically, it can break the helix structure of the chromosome. Repair is possible, but sometime it does no repair. This is an epigenetic effect. The build up of IR over time, or exposure to higher doses of IR can cause cancer. When fission occurs, cells divide and a mutation type cell is often present in both cells. When these cells do not die, IR can often cause changes in proteins, thereby distorting cell growth. This often leads to the formation of groups of cancer cells, called tumors.

In summary, ionizing radiation involves physics. IR causes electrons within the body to be lost or added onto different molecules within the body. This can be described as mutations within the body. The magnitude, the type, as well as the duration, of ionizing radiation, can all be an incentive for cancer in the long term. One must respect even the smallest amount of ionizing radiation.

4.2) Sources of Ionizing Radiation

Electrons vibrate due to ionizing energy. Gamma rays have the highest energy, with the next highest being X - rays. They both knock electrons off an atom or isotope. Some frequencies of UV light are ionizing. Specifically, when the wave length of the light is 100nm, that is 100 nano meters or less ,it is ionizing. Radioactivity is the spontaneous release of energy from an atom which is unstable. Again, atoms with the same atomic number of equal or different mass are called isotopes. Only a single isotope of an atom appears on a conventional periodic table of elements. In fact, they have the same number of protons as an atom described in the periodic table, but their atomic mass number may differ. Radioactive decay is the process of an atom emitting radiation to become more and more stable. Most elements within the periodic table are stable. Some exceptions to this are described next.

Primordial atoms are radioactive atoms which occur naturally, and can be mined. They are atoms sometimes described in the Periodic Table of Elements, PTE, proper. For instance, Thorium 232, Uranium 238, and Potassium 40, K40 are primordial atoms. However, only the first two isotopes are on the PTE. Observing the periodic table, Potassium 39, K39 is stable with 19 protons and 20 neutrons. However, occurring naturally, one in 10,000 Potassium atoms have an atomic mass of 40 which makes them unstable.

Cosmic rays help produce Carbon 14, C14 which is also radioactive. It has six protons and eight neutrons. On the PTE is C13, which is not radioactive. Because the human body has lots of carbon, a small amount of C14 appears in the body, thereby making human bodies somewhat radioactive. Cesium 137 is a man made radioactive atom. It occurs as a byproduct of fission within nuclear reactors. Electricity can also generate radioactive elements. Among the most popular are X ray and CAT, Computer Axial Tomography. An in-depth description of CAT can be found in (Giardina, 2025).

4.3) Types of Ionizing Radiation

Radiation occurs in the process of a radioactive element becoming more and more stable. Radiation can occur in one step, or several steps for stability, or it may never occur, as in Bismuth, Bi. At each step, the resulting element becomes more and more stable. However, at each step from the beginning, only radioactive isotopes are involved. Only the last result in the process results in a stable atom, and as such can always be found in the periodic table. Example 4.1 provided below, illustrates the large number of steps, required until stability is achieved. In this instance, exactly eleven radiating events convert Uranium 235 into Lead 207. The last element, Pb207 is stable.

There are four types of radiation emitted from a radioactive element: alpha particles, α ; beta particles, β; gamma rays, γ; and neutron emission, n. In chemical equations the neutron particle is often denoted as H^+. In this case H is the Hydrogen atom and H^+, is the positive ion, also called a cation. Alpha particles travel up to an inch in the air, and cannot penetrate a piece of paper or clothing, or even skin. They consist of two protons and two neutrons, like a helium atom. Under alpha decay, the new atoms have a decreased atomic number by two, and a decreased mass by four. Beta particles can travel up to about 10 feet, and can be blocked by thick plastic. These particles can go through skin and cause skin burns. Beta decay can be viewed as the release of an electron or positron. In the former case, the resulting atom has an increased single proton, and loss of a neutron. In the latter decay, an exchange of proton for a neutron occurs. In both cases, there are no changes in mass. Gamma rays travel many yards in the air, and can be blocked by inches of lead. These rays are photons or electrical waves, and therefore, do not produce changes in the atomic number or mass. Finally, neutrons can be discharged as a form of radiation. All forms of decay are very detrimental to internal digestion.

Due to the positive charge inherent within an alpha particle, it can knock off electrons from a collision with another element. Because of this, it is strongly ionizing. The beta particle, however, is weakly ionizing. When the beta particle is an electron, it is symbolized as just β, and in some documents, by e or as β^-. The resulting isotope is a cation. However, when an isotope loses a hole or a positron, the loss is symbolized using β^+. The resulting isotope is a negative ion, also called an anion.. A single step of alpha radiation, and beta radiation are symbolized respectively by:

$-\alpha$—>, and $-\beta$—>.

Additionally, a positive integer k, may appear in front of α, or β. This positive integer, implies k values of alpha radiation, or beta radiation respectively occur. Again, the symbologies are kα, and kβ.

Example 4.1) (Moore, and Stanitiski, 2014).

Radiation can occur in eleven steps for the Uranium 235 isotope, through which it becomes stable Lead 207. The sequence of successive radiation emissions is given by: α, β, α, β, α, α, α, α, β, β, α. Equivalently, it can be given by: α, β, α, β, 4α, 2 β, α. The specific sequence of isotopes losing ionizing radiation is: $^{235}_{92}$U $-\alpha$—> Thorium 231, $^{231}_{90}$Th$-\beta$—> Protactinium 231, $^{231}_{91}$Pr$-\alpha$—>Actinium 227, $^{227}_{89}$Ac $-\beta$—> Thorium 227, $^{227}_{90}$Th$-\alpha$—>Radium 223, $^{223}_{88}$Ra $-\alpha$—> Radon 219, $^{219}_{86}$Rn$-\alpha$—>Polonium 215, $^{215}_{84}$Po$-\alpha$—>Lead 211, $^{211}_{82}$Pb$-\beta$—> Bismuth 211,

$^{211}_{83}$Bi—β—-> Polonium 211, $^{211}_{84}$Po—α—> Lead 207, $^{207}_{82}$Pb.#

4.4) Ionizing Radioactive Contamination

Contamination occurs when radioactive material settles on clothing, or the hair, or the body. This is external contamination. Often the radiation can be removed by removing and washing the clothing. When inhaled, or through digestion, the radioactive material causes very harmful internal contamination. It can ionize molecules within the body, and even make them break apart. Reactive species can alter the structure of surrounding molecules and can mutate the DNA.

Civilian nuclear power reactors and plants used for electricity generation should be abolished. Traditional gas, oil, coal, hydro and other non nuclear methods for electricity generation need only be employed. More than enough nuclear emissions and waste materials occur by way of necessary national defense applications. Additionally, employment of nuclear for medical and research applications are needed. There is no purpose in proliferating forever lasting, invisible toxins and pollution. Continuation of nuclear development should be encouraged, but not for the sake of the energy greedy AI bunch.

Ionizing radiation produces enough energy to cause the ejection of electrons from atoms. Equivalently, it can provide additional electrons to attach to an atom. Ionizing radiation principally occurs from nuclear emissions and waste products. Emitted are alpha and beta particles, as well as high frequency gamma rays. All these emissions are harmful to the DNA of the human body. The radiation might directly injure the DNA. It could also alter the DNA indirectly. In brief, free radicals can form. Specifically, the body is made up of mostly water, and contact with these particles or waves can modify the water atoms. In this case, water, H_2O molecules are transformed into the following molecules: Hydrogen, H; And, hydroxyls, OH; As well as hydrogen superoxide, HO_2; Also occurring is H_2, dihydrogen: Or even hydrogen peroxide, H_2O_2. (NRC.gov, 2014). The absolute amount of radiation is inversely proportional to the half life of the radiating source.

There is an over abundance of units to determine the degree of ionizing radiation, as well as how and where it is measured. In the following, many distinct units which provide the amount of radiation are listed. In this listing, unit preferences are mentioned.

Hopefully, they indicate the more common and useful units. Following the brief listing of units, there exist in-depth descriptions of all the units as well as conditions for measurements. Additionally, their meaning is described in depth, along with conversions involving units. Illustrations are also provided:

The first set of units are Becquerels, Bq, and more importantly, Counts Per Second, CPS, which provide the amount of radiation emitted from a radio active source.

The next set of units are C/kg, and of more interest is the Roentgen, R. These units describe exposure, providing a measure of the amount of radiation traveling through the air.

The next set of units are the Radiation Absorption Rate, RAD. More importantly, Grays, Gy, are used. These units are employed to give the amount of radiation absorbed in tissue.

Finally, the units which take into account the type of ionizing radioactivity entering the tissue are given in units of Roentgen Equivalent for Man, REM, and of more importance, Sieverts, Sv. These units provide the effective dose to the tissue.

The amount of ionizing radiation emitted from a radio active material, that is, coming directly from the source, is measured in units of Becquerel Bq. It is one radioactivity event per second, that is, one radioactive emission disintegration in a second. This quantity is also specified in Counts Per Second, CPS. This number tells us how many atoms in the material decay in a given time period. It does not distinguish whether the emission is an alpha particle, a beta particle, gamma ray, X - ray or a neutron. It provides the radioactivity directly from the source in a given time period.

One ten inch banana has about 12 Bq = 12 CPS, of radioactive activity. This is due to the radioactive Potassium within. The radioactive Potassium is the isotope 40. The most radioactive food is the Brazil nut. It contains high levels of both Radium and Potassium. Radium occurs in the ground, resulting in the root system of an edible substance absorbing this element. For Brazil nuts having about the same weight as the banana, the amount of radiation in a Brazil nut is double that of the banana. An older unit for measuring the amount of radioactivity, that is, the rate of ionizing radiation directly from the source, is the Curie, C. C describes a large amount of radiation, the conversion into units of Becquerel is one C equals 37,000 million Bq. (NRC.gov, 2020).

Exposure provides a measure of the amount of radiation traveling through the air. The units for exposure are the Roentgen, R and the Coulomb, C per Kilogram, kg, that is, C/kg. A Coulomb is the amount of electric charge carried by a current of one amp flowing in one second. One kilogram, kg equals 2.2046 pounds, lbs. The ambient radiation level measures the ionizing radiation in the environment; it is source number plus background. Usually, this quantity is used when there is no deliberate, or explicit source of ionizing radiation introduced. The ambient radiation is also referred to as the background radiation. Radiation monitors such as the Mazur 9000 measures exposure in terms of Roentgen, R.

The unit R is often employed in measuring background ionizing radiation. The value of background radiation depends on numerous factors, for instance, the altitude. As an illustration, for some cities in Colorado, the value of background radiation is .022mR/hr. That is, .022 mili Roentgens per hour. While in Miami Florida, the value would be .012mR/hr. For an airplane cruising 40,000 feet above ground the reading for individuals within would be about 400mR/hr or equivalently .4R/hr. (Mazur, 2017). More information can be found in (U.S.NRC, 2021). For instance, persons who receive an additional annual amount of radiation from breathing air due to Radon, adds 200mR. While if a person wears a Plutonium-powered cardiac pacemaker, the additional value is 100mR.

The amount of radiation absorbed in tissue is calculated in units of Grays Gy per hour, Gy/hour. This is an absorption rate and is also given by units of RAD, which is the Radiation Absorption Rate. One gray equals 100 RAD, Gy = 100RAD. More rigorously, One Gy equals one Joule of ionizing energy deposited on one kilogram of human tissue. Again one kilogram, kg equals 2.2046 pounds lbs. A Joule, J equals one Newton, N times one Meter, m. One Newton equals one kilogram times meter divided by second quantity squared, that is s squared. A meter equals 39.37 inches. Additionally, one RAD equals .01 joules of energy deposited per kilogram of tissue. This unit is more common in medical applications. (NRC.gov, 2020)

The dose equivalent is also called the effective dose. It is usually a term referring to the medical effects of absorption in the tissue of specific ionizing radiation. The units in this case take into account the types of ionizing radiation. Both beta particle type radiation, and gamma or X-ray type radiation are equivalent, as far as the absorbed dose is concerned. Whereas, alpha particle and neutron radiation are more damaging to the human body, they also have equivalent dose absorption parameters. These parameters are given by the Relative Biological Effectiveness, RBE. For beta particles, gamma and X rays, RBE = one. However, for alpha particle and neutron radiation RBE = ten. (RREM, 2025).

Units of Sieverts, Sv/hour, provides the dose equivalent to the gray value. The Sv unit takes into account the type of radiation for instance alpha, beta particles, or X-rays, and gamma rays. The formula is, Sievert equals Gray times RBE. The other unit for dose equivalence is the Roentgen Equivalent for Man, REM. The conversion factor in this case is One Sievert, equals one hundred REM. It follows that, REM equals RAD times RBE. *There is no safe amount of exposure to ionizing radiation.*

In practice, exposure of 1R equals an absorbed dose of one RAD, equals a dose equivalent of one REM. (NRC.gov, 2020).

Milli sieverts units are usually employed, mSv/hour or even micro sieverts per hour. The recommended maximum exposure for whole body dose is 3 - 50 mSv per year. A body dose of 5000mSv gives a 1/2 probability of death within sixty days. A larger dose leads to acute radiation poisoning. Poisoning occurs in four phases:

Prodromal

Latent Period

Manifest Illness Stage

Late Effects, Somatic and Genetic, Recovery, Cancer or Death

Radiation exposure of 1- 10 Gy causes bone marrow disease and kills white, red blood cells as well as platelets. For more than 10 Gy, the GI tract is effected. In this case, the body cannot absorb nutrients, and death is certain. When more than 20 Gy of exposure occurs, the brain cannot control body functions due to cell death.

4.5) Useful Measurements For Determining Radiation Amounts

Compared to obtaining instantaneous radiation measurements, readings taken over periods of time are often more important. Various types of descriptive statistical information can be employed over a specified period of time. Among the units used are: Counts per second, CPS; Counts per minute, CPM; Milli Roentgen per hour, mR/hr; Micro Roentgen per hour, μ R/hr; And finally, micro Sieverts per hour, μSv/hr.

Among the most important are the average measurement, the maximum value attained, or the minimum value of radiation over the given time period. A useful provision is to time tag the point at which maximum, or minimum values of ionizing radiation occurred. Specifying the date at which the measurements are taken, is often an important feature. Another measurement of importance is the total count determined over a specific period of time.

Example 4.2)

Suppose that a nuclear radiation monitor is employed in determining the average background radiation using units of milli Roentgen per hour. Assume these measurements are taken over a period of two full days and three hours. If the reading over this period of time is .030mR/hr, and then the total accumulated dose is easily found. It is 51hr x .030mR/hr = 1.53mR.#

5) Role of Mitochondria in Cancer

5.1) DNA Description

DNA is an abbreviation for the chemical Deoxyribo Nucleic Acid. It is a polymer, that is, a large molecule comprised of many smaller molecules. It is a double helix type ladder structure, and its normal state consists of a compactly constructed structure. DNA are compressed to fit within the nucleus of a cell. If untangled it is about six feet in length, and consists of 46 sections or chromosomes. However only 23 different types exist and each appear as a compressed spring. The two chromosomes which are the same are called chromosome pairs. Each pair is created by both the mother and the father. The last pair are called the sex chromosomes. If the last chromosome pair is XY, then it is indicative of a male. When this pair is XX, this denotes a female. Genes are short segments of chromosomes that provides codes for a specific gene.

Genome is the entire set of genetic material. Amino acids are chemical molecules within the body that combine to form proteins. In short, they break down food and create proteins. There are about twenty types of amino acids having distinct shape. Amino acids consist of atoms: Oxygen, O; Carbon, C; Hydrogen, H; Nitrogen, N. Sometimes they also contain Sulfur, S; Phosphorous, P. Ions from these atoms also might appear. Amino acids exist within the cell in the cytoplasm. The cytoplasm is mostly a fluid area within the membranes of a cell, but it also contains the small organs within the cell. It does not refer to the nucleus when a nucleus exists, but it does include mitochondria. DNA provides a script how the amino acids should combine to provide specific proteins. There are millions of different proteins. Each consisting of a polypeptide chain of amino acids. A strand of DNA consists of millions of nucleotides.

Transcription occurs by making partial copies of DNA called RNA. They look similar to DNA but are shorter length strings, and they consist of one side of the ladder structure. Additionally, in the case of RNA the nucleotides are labeled A, G, C, and U. In order, these labels are abbreviations for the following acid bases: adenine, guanine, cytosine and uracil, respectively. These act bases occur mainly in the nucleus. They travel to the cytoplasm, and, because they are narrow, they can pass through pours in the nucleus and through the boundary of the cytoplasm. Subsequently, they appear in the ribosome. It is here that protein is created three nucleotides at a time. This construct is referred to as a codon.

In more depth, cells within the body consists of three parts, the cell membrane which forms the exterior boundary, the inner annuli part called the cytoplasm, and the innermost nucleus. The cytoplasm refers to fluid which fills the cell, but it includes proteins, amino acids and as organelles. The nucleus is the cell's control center. Most of the time, it is here that the DNA exists. Four acid bases exist within the DNA, similar to RNA. In this case they are abbreviated C, G, A, and T; the first three were specified previously, but here the last basis is thymine. These are chemically sugar and phosphate molecules. Therefore, they consist of H, O, C and N. They appear as a sequence within a double helix spiral comprising the DNA. The pairings are A and T, also G and C. See Figure 5.1A.

Phosphate forms the backbone for the DNA. Chromosomes carry the DNA within the nucleus of the cell when the nucleus exists. A small amount of DNA appears in the mitochondria. This DNA is abbreviated mtDNA. Mitochondria convert potential energy into kinetic energy. This happens within all cells except perhaps blood cells. The mtDNA is further described below. Each DNA string consists of 146 base elements compressed into a small volume. However, the DNA is made up of about a billion bases elements within the whole body. As noted a single string is about six feet in length, so in order to fit within a cell's nucleus this string is tightly wrapped around numerous histones. Histones are described in more depth next.

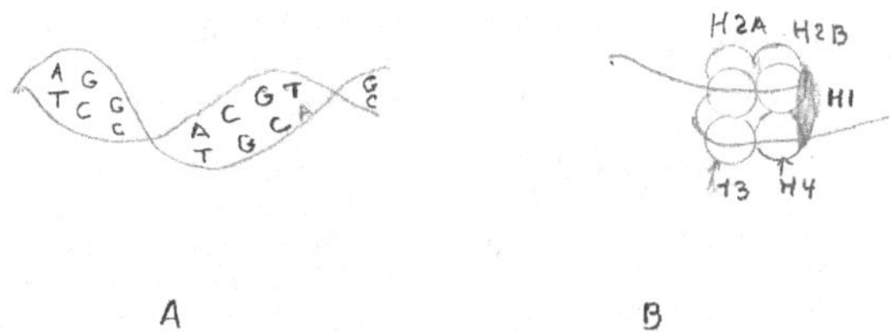

FIGURE 5.1) DNA and Histone

All the cells within a human body contain the same DNA sequence, however there are distinct epigenetic modifications within a cell. Epigenetic means on top of genetics and refer to external modifications of the DNA. Epigenetic are said to interpret DNA. It turns genes on and off and describes changes in gene expression which are not encoded within the actual DNA sequence. These modifications do not change the DNA sequence but involve various types of epigenetic regulators to describe gene transcription. Regulators are non coded RNA, also more specifically methylation modification, and histone modification.

5.2) Methylation and Histone Modification of DNA

Methylation modification and histone modification enable the creation of distinct cell types, such as skin, kidney, muscle and so on. They also prohibit certain modifications from occurring, and might reverse previously made modifications. Epigenetic modifications occur as a result of aging, drugs, diet, and environment, in particular, in response to toxins such as ionizing radiation.

RNA polymerase, that is Ribo Nucleic Acid Polymerase, RNAP, is an enzyme which, with the help of other proteins, binds itself to a specific part of the DNA. It provides the transcription process. This is itself a catalyst, and needs no starting or stopping conditions. (B D Editors, 2019). In short, the transcription process maps DNA into RNA and this is translated into proteins. The mappings are:

DNA———>RNA———->Protein.

DNA methylation is the process in which DNA is not in the active state of replication.

Methylation modification is the process by which methyl molecules attaches itself to DNA. This is the normal state. It occurs 75% of the time. A methyl molecule consists of a Carbon atom which bonds with three Hydrogen atoms. When present, this prevents certain gene expression to turn on or to turn off. When the methyl molecule is attached, it usually attaches to C or G, also called a CpG island. This occurs because C and G have more bonds, namely three, instead of two for A or T. High DNA methylation ensures inactivate DNA transcription, it is a defense mechanism. Un-methylation DNA can make cancer or bacteria more likely. In short, high methylation prevents RNA to form, thus

DNA—-x—>RNA—x—>protein.

Histones have interior units as well as an exterior structure with the latter histone designated H1. H1 is the largest unit, and most important protein. It holds the interior units together. It binds the Histones and enables DNA condensed wrapping. The interior histone units have two of each H2A, H2B, H3, and H4 protein. See Figure 5.1.B. Histones are positively charged, and this enhances the binding with the negatively charged DNA. Modifications do occur, and involves epigenetic factors which relax the tightly wound DNA. This can be thought of as the open state, and it is called histone acetylation. It enables proteins to be read from the genes. DNA tightly wrapped around histones cannot be read by the cell. This can be thought of as the more usual common closed state. It makes accidental transcription less likely. That is, de-acetylation makes transcription much less likely because the DNA is wrapped tightly. When the chromosome is relaxed, there is a higher chance of cancer occurring. Over acting de-acetylation leads to gene silencing; it cannot transcribe at all. In short, de-acetylation enables DNA to not be mapped into RNA, so,

DNA —-x—>RNA—-x—->protein.

Genes are sequences of DNA. Specifically, and previously mentioned, a codon is a triple of base elements. Gene mutation can occur when one nucleotide is changed, inserted or deleted, producing an erroneous protein. (Tatomir, 2024). Living organisms have genes which determine the amino acids and proteins within the body.

5.3) Major Types of Ionizing Radiation

To begin, a simple type of mutation is described next. It involves low frequency UV light of wave length 120nm to 400nm. Thymine and Cytosine cross linking forms a kink in the DNA, the RNA cannot be formed, and transcription is thus impossible. In this case, protein cannot stop dividing the cell due to mutation.

We do not have enough true statistically sound data to make very meaningful conclusions about the cause of cancer when a small, say one milli sievert of exposure, exists. (ICRP Publication 99, p 27). This is because most statistical data sets are too small. But there are numerous cases for IR causing cancer. Appendix 3 provides a survey of nuclear situations and incidents of cancer caused by ionizing radiation. An example is provided by the radium dial worker's situation. Upon death, studies showed cancers occurred because they painted numbers using Radium, Ra. These workers deposited Radium on numerous objects, mostly clocks and watches. The workers often licked the brushes containing Ra. This element emitted the most deadly particles - alpha particles. This resulted in bone marrow disease, namely cancer. In response to this event, the first occupational radioactive guide was subsequently published. It specified about .6 milli grays per week type limitations on workers. This converts to about a milli sievert per week. The limit is hopefully enforced for uranium miners. It, too, should hold for medical workers as well as for persons breathing radon in homes and other dwellings.

The short term effects from IR is acute radiation sickness and usually death due to rapid cell death in a short time. There exist four phases. This does not include massive IR, because death in such case often occurs immediately:

A) Prodromal phase - symptoms occur in hours, or in up to 3 days. Symptoms that may or may not be experienced include headache, vomiting, diarrhea and high fever,

B) Latent phase - apparent recovery, but lab tests show serious changes in the blood and lymph nodes. Here, tests often indicate the amount of radiation that occurred.

C) Manifest illness phase - cells try to rid themselves of infection, hair might fall out, and there is disorientation

D) Final phase - death or recovery

These phases depend upon the dosage of IR:

For dose less than 1.5 Gy, the phases A) - C) hold for about one day to several weeks, and phase D) is likely to result in full recovery;

For a dose of 1.5 - 4 Gy, phase D) results in possible recovery with supportive hospital care;

For an exposure of 4 - 5 Gy, phase D) has a conclusion of certain death absent of supportive care;

For a dose 5 - 15 Gy, phase D) results in a low probability of recovery even with supportive care;

For a dose of IR more than 15 Gy death occurs within 48 hours.

The ICRP publication 99 provides data on the long term cancer effects from IR. In particular, it describes the atomic and nuclear bomb survivor data cancer risk. A life span study involving 79,901 people, who survived both the Hiroshima and Nagasaki bombs, is provided in (Pierce and Preston, 2000). These statistics give the estimated number of IR associated cancers as a function of the dose and also the exposure distance. An instance of a result within the report is given for some 3,048 survivors. These subjects were exposed to one - half to one Gy, and they had 582 solid cancers, while 177 were estimated to have IR associated excess cancers. Long term effects, often called delayed somatic effects, included cancers, mutations and birth defects.

5.4) Cancer and the Mitochondrial Disfunction Due to Ionizing Radiation

Cellular metabolism and health integrity of cells are regulated by the mitochondria. There exist on average about 2,000 mitochondria within a cell. The mitochondria alone occupy from one twentyth to one quarter of the cells volume. Each mitochondria converts potential energy into kinetic energy. The potential energy involves glucose, oxygen, water as well as amino and fatty acids. The kinetic energy is used in powering the cells, along with inter and intra cell signaling of other mitochondria, and as a heat source. Where more energy is needed, like within muscle cells, and in particular the heart, hundreds of thousands of mitochondria can exists within each cell. Using electronic transport signaling, they produce ATP, referring to the site of oxidative phosphorylation. ATP is the energy generated, standing for Adenosine TriphosPhate. Cells increase the number of mitochondria during cell growth as well as fission, which is the property of splitting apart. This was previously mentioned in Section 3.1, along with fusion, whereby two distinct mitochondria join together to form an elongated interconnected structure, and share their information. Fission and fusion can be considered as two aspects of mitochondrial quality control. In particular, fission can be thought of as a repair process. Fission by products are the creation of normal mitochondria. (Su, et al, 2023). Some reports say that the lens within the eyes, as well as red blood cells, have no mitochondria. (Lenzen, 2014), (Helmenstine, 2024). On the other hand, some scientists reportedly found mitochondria within human blood. (Lazaro, 2025).

Mitochondria contain their own DNA. This DNA is denoted as mtDNA. There are between two and ten copies of mtDNA within each mitochondria. Its purpose is similar to the DNA within the nuclease of a cell. It is a double stranded and circular molecule with 16,569 base pairs. However, there are two more striking differences from the nucleus DNA. First, only the mother's DNA is utilized in this structure. More importantly, the histone protection described in Section 5.2 is totally absent in the mtDNA. A consequence is that the natural state, the closed state of protected DNA, is not present in mtDNA. The latter DNA is not histone tightly compressed, it is wide open, inviting IR to hit it. This open state insures that the mtDNA is more prone to damaging agents. Mitochondrial dysfunction can arise from IR and a result can be cancer.

The effect of IR can be better understood by relating the process in which ATP is transmitted. Indeed, signals are sent using the Electron Transport Chain, ETC within the mitochondria. This chain is comprised of protein clusters. The protein clusters transfer electrons thru membranes within the mitochondria. The overall goal is the creation of kinetic energy in the form of ATP. This occurs by the forming of a proton gradient. The process is referred to as OXPHOS, or OXidative PHOSphorylation. During OXPHOS, between one percent to five percent of electrons leak out the mitochondria's boundaries. These are the inner and outer membranes.

Recall that IR is typified as a type of radiation which disturbs electrons. (Rong, et al, 2021). (Averbeck, and Rodriguer-Lafrasse, 2020). In the last reference it is explained how the dose and quality of IR harms the mtDNA. Moreover, IR affects all parts of the cell. Mitochondria disfunction effects DNA transcription, translation, regulation of expression and protein activation. Additionally, the mtDNA has less ability for self repair than nuclear DNA. Mitochondria have 37 genes encoding for 13 proteins. These all are involved in OXPHOS. Furthermore, mitochondria have little or no repair type genes nor do they have proliferative type genes. (Leija, et al, 2017).

It also has been reported that gamma radiation showed a higher level of DNA methylation problems, resulting in various cancers. (Averbeck, and Rodriguer-Lafrasse, 2020). In this report the authors identify more than 500 references.

IR also produces higher Reactive Oxygen Species, ROS, and oxidative stress, thereby causing mitochondrial dysfunction. This again often results in various cancers. Oxidative stress is described below in terms of free radicals. In the last listed reference it is explained how IR causes mtDNA damage. The result often in cell death from DNA nucleotide deletion, as explained in Section 5.2. Moreover, even low levels of IR induce slight mitochondria dysfunction, involving fusion and fission. However, higher levels of IR, for instance when heavy ions are present, resulting in cell death. In the reference, there are in depth descriptions of the types of IR, and how they relate to different cancers within the human body. These concepts are also described in terms of mitochondria dysfunction. Effects of alpha particles leading to gene mutations are presented in this reference. In any case, the AI CANCER TIMEBOMB follows.

Reduced atoms are atoms which gain one or more electrons, and are called an anion. On the other hand if an atom losses an electron and become positively charged it is said to be oxidized and is a cation. These are the two distinct types of charged ions. In metabolic type processes there are free radicals; these are positively charged ions, that is, they are cations. Anti-oxidants cling to positive radicals, resulting in non charged molecules. Free radicals are cations. Anti-oxidants are anions. During cellular respiration small amounts of free radicals escape the mitochondria. They can attack proteins lipids in blood cells, as well as in DNA. This results in cell damage and can cause cancer. This is a common occurrence is when there are too many free radicals. The overall process is called oxidative stress.

5.5) Ending on a Happier Note

This section largely presents the work of Dr Seyfried. (Seyfried, 2015). A summary, of his thesis is that all cancers are the same metabolic disease. Metabolic diseases are the chemical and electrical processes which occur in the body to convert food into kinetic energy. Subsequently, building blocks for cells are created. All cancers are caused by dysfunction of the mitochondria. Specifically, in all cancers, the conversion from potential energy into kinetic energy is performed without oxygen. The mitochondria resorts to fermentation instead of oxygen in this conversion. Cancer cells adapt to fermentation and instead of dying, they proliferate in a deregulated cell growth.

Dr Seyfried found that for the survival of cancer, the essential, and unique, fuels needed by the mitochondria are glucose, and the non-essential amino acid, glutamine. Restriction of these two substances kills the cancer. However, total restriction of glutamine would kill the human. The basic idea for cancer resolution is to minimize glucose intake, and induce ketosis. Afterwards, a non toxic glutamine substitute is given to the patient. It is applied in a pulse modulating manner. The application is performed for a specified time, and at a designated frequency. A frequent result is shrinking of the tumors as well as tumor isolation. Thereafter, application of non-toxic hyperbaric oxygen, or mild radiation is performed. The former treatment is well known, (Mills, 1978). Additional specifics are provided below.

Diet and lifestyle have a great impact on controlling the occurrence of cancer. People have control over diet and lifestyle. But not over the environment. There is no control over the amount of toxins, such as IR, and nuclear particles that exist in the ground, in our food and in the atmosphere. Presently, there is a world wide epidemic of cancer. One half of the population is predicted tone stricken by cancer in their life time. In the US alone, 1,700 people a day die of cancer. This equates to 70 US citizens dying from cancer per hour and the death rate is going up.

Dr Seyfried's discovery is premised on the Warburg effect. The Warburg effect relates that a cancerous cell's production of ATP is generated by glycolysis, in place of OXPHOS. Glycolysis is the process through which sugar is broken down by cells. This occurs in an enzyme reaction that needs little or no oxygen. Glycolysis can be harmful because it yields low amounts of kinetic energy. However, it is the only energy source which can be used by red blood cells.

See the last reference, which refers to a proton gradient. Also see, the following references for the Warburg effect. (Warburg, 1956). (Rao, 2016). Warburg essentially said 80% of cancers could be reduced by minimizing the use of glucose. However, the opening of more and more nuclear plants provides a new catalyst for the AI CANCER TIMEBOMB, negating Warburg's hopes.

The following few paragraphs are edited additional scientific and summary facts provided by (Seyfried, 2024). Cancer mutations in DNA are caused by mitochondria disfunction. Fermenting glutamine and glucose cause this disfunction. Fermentation is carried out in the absence of oxygen. During this process there is an exchange of electrons between molecules. Contaminants in the atmosphere such as IR do not help matters. Metabolic homeostases is the state of good heath, and is controlled mainly by the mitochondria. Every cancer exhibits disfunction of mitochondria due to fermentation. Cancer is cell division out of control, because there is mitochondria dysfunction. Mitochondria can no longer control the halt of fermentation. Plus, the higher the intake of sugar, the faster cancer will grow.

Fermentation produces energy in a slow manner. The fuels, that is the potential energies, are glutamine and glucose. Glutamine is an amino acid; it is most abundant within the blood cells. It is a non-essential amino acid, that is it is manufactured by the body. Glutamine is also needed for digestion, the cognitive function and immune health. Fatty acids and ketone bodies can be used by heathy cells, but not by cancer cells. Cancer is a symptom of problems within the mitochondria. Glucose has carbons and produces lactic acid as tumor secretions. Glutamine contains nitrogen and hydrogen, it is an amino acid. Together, glucose and glutamine produce fermentation and drive a rapid proliferation of cancer cells.

By using diet and lifestyle changes, glucose can be minimized. Dr. Atkinson's diet, or Keto diets, can be employed to minimize carbohydrates. However, the Atkinson diet does not minimize proteins. Proteins contain glutamine. This is a potential problem for two reasons; glutamine itself feeds tumors, also, proteins reduce to carbohydrates after time. This is why the the Keto diet is preferred. In any case, it is possible to kill cancer cells by removing sugar, and controlling glutamine. This can occur with or without toxins such as chemo or IR. Cancer immunotherapy is now focusing on glutamine. (Wang, et al, 2024).

In a healthy cell, insulin, glucose and oxygen, OxPhos gives off Carbon dioxide, CO_2 and water, H_2 0. Cancer cells take in glucose and glutamine and they give off lactate, and succinate, respectively. The way to stop cancer is by stopping the intake of glucose, and periodically halting the intake of glutamine. A modulation technique introduces pulse therapy, to turn on and turn off the body's production of glutamine. The basic idea is first, to try to make ketone bodies. Cancer cells cannot use ketones as a source of potential energy. (Seyfried, et al, 2020). Hyperbaric oxygen is used instead of toxins. This is performed after the state of ketosis is achieved together with the pulse moderation treatment of a glutamine inhibitor.

Numerous experiments were conducted with and without glucose. These are in vitro tests, that is using test tubes. These experiments were performed to find all amino acids which enable cancer to persist. The result was that only glutamine enabled cancer to continue with or without glucose. With or without oxygen, when glutamine only is used, ATP is produced. Labeled glutamine was used to demonstrate that labeled succinate acid resulted, proving fermentation metabolism is utilized. (Seyfried, 2025), (Duraj, et al, 2024).

To manage cancer, the body must only operate on fatty acids and ketones, because cancer will not survive on those. DON drugs are designed to starve cancer cells by substituting DONs for glutamine. In short, DONs are used as inhibitors for glutamine. DON stands for the anticancer drug, 6-Diazo-5-Oxo-L-Norleucine. These drugs are employed when glucose is not present. DONs stop all metabolic pathways which use glutamine. (Huang, 2022).

AI) A.I. and Control Systems

A1.1) AI Background and Closed Loop Systems

The term AI is attributed to Prof. John McCarthy. He came up with the term at a work shop on thinking machines, at Dartmouth College in 1956, (Coursera staff, 2024).

The country has come a long way since President Donald Trump declared the Artificial Intelligence, AI initiative in 2019. (Trump, D., 2019). His ingenuity ensured that the U.S. became a leader in safe, secure, reliable, and innovative AI. President Trump's leadership in AI had a direct effect on manufacturing, leading the development of robotic systems as well as popularizing self driving vehicles. These initiatives have had important impacts in medical improvements, such as wearable health devices and precision medicine utilizing deep learning. Benefits of these initiatives have also been felt in national defense, and space command, as well as in finance and climate predictions.

Sad to say, the subsequent administration's contribution was principally engendering an AI scare, and undoing many of the scientific benefits of these disciplines. Every other word from the past administration was a caution for responsible artificial intelligence use, and its dangers. Moreover, this administration demanded a call for validation for efficacy, trustworthiness and social fairness. Additionally, after President Trump's first term there was aways reference for safeguarding consumer privacy. Additionally, there were demands for penalties and disclosure requirements for the utilization of emerging AI in election messaging.

To demonize AI is insane; it is like demonizing guns. The object of wickedness should be ascribed to the creator of an evil AI program or algorithm. Similarly, evilness should be attributed to a human shooter with bad intentions, and not to the inanimate object used. AI has no political implications. This discipline is a diversified mixture of basic mathematics, physics, engineering concepts and computer science. AI is best explained as the interplay between sensors, computers and control surfaces operating in a closed loop fashion. Within the computers, algorithms are specified with parameters determined from domain knowledge. Alternately, these parameters are inferred by using learning techniques, such as neural networks. The sensors collect data, which are sent to computers for smoothing, filtering and prediction purposes. Subsequent signals are transmitted to control surfaces, usually in the form of electrical currents. AI results are manifested through information conveyed decisions made, as well as manipulations of the surrounds. These functions are performed in accordance with human objectives. Humans may or may not be part of the closed loop system. However, they are almost always involved in the creation of initial conditions, as well as AI objectives.

AI is the structured development of theory, methodology and physical systems that enable computers and robots to perform tasks that historically have been judged to lie within the domain of intelligence. (Dougherty and Giardina, 1988).

The term 'artificial intelligence' means a machine-based system that can, for a given set of human-defined objectives, generate information, provide solutions, make predictions, recommendations, or decisions influencing real, or virtual environments. All of these operations are performed in a timely manner. (Wikapeadia, 2024)

For years the U.S. Department of Defense, DOD has utilized Fire and Forget weaponry. Here, initial information about targets are pre-programmed into the weapon, usually a missile. After this, and without human intervention, the weapon travels without Line of Sight, LOS. Also, without target illumination or wire guidance, it ultimately hits the target. In this situation, usually the AI closed loop system does not involve further human guidance. Among the possible sensors are Global Positioning System, GPS, as well as Inertial Navigation Systems, INS. The latter system involves accelerators, ring laser gyroscopes and altimeters. Radar and inferred optics are also often utilized.

A similar AI closed loop concept is TERCOM, short for TERain COntour Matching. Here, contour maps are preloaded or learnt from satellite transmissions. Similar to fire and forget devices, human intervention is not needed. Usually these AI robots are cruise missiles. They employ INS as well as radar altimeters to correlate observed data with pre-stored data. The stored data usually is in the form of imagery. These missiles fly low and stay within the atmosphere. Unlike ballistic missiles which have rockets and can leave the atmosphere in order to hit their target.

A1.2) Open Loop Systems

In commercial plane flights the use of INS and Global Navigation Satellite Systems, GNSS are widely used. For instance, GPS illustrates some typical types of sensors employed in this environment. In this case, the human usually is part of the closed loop AI system. After the initial condition of routing and taking off, the various sensors send observation type data signals to the computer. These signals represent latitude, longitude and altitude as well as speed and orientation. Within the computer, fusion type algorithms, such as the Kalman Filters, are utilized in providing a best estimate of the true location of the craft. This information can be sent to the pilot for approval. If sent, it is revealed to the pilot using control surfaces in the form of video or audio synthesizer. The pilot's brain interprets the information; this takes the place of a computer.

When the craft is on course, the pilot could touch a control screen for confirmation that all is well. Simultaneously, electrical signals representing estimated navigational information are sent from the computer to control surfaces. These are engines, the ailerons, elevators, and rudders. The latter three surfaces control the lateral balance or roll motion, the pitch and yaw motion of the craft respectively. When the pilot receives indications that the craft is off course, a manual adjustment to these control surfaces can be conducted. Signals are sent to control surfaces involving voice commands or by using pressure sensors. Here, the human closes the control loop.

More common, and timely applications of AI are found with generative AI wherein a human being is almost always part of the closed loop control system. Indeed, in these cases the human closes the loop. The AI robotic aid is itself an open loop system. A human would interface with a robot aid by asking for answers to questions or asking for advice. Additionally, certain movements or changes in the environment might be desired from the robotic aid. For instance, when appropriate sensors and control surfaces are present, change or adjustment to the temperature within a room might be needed. Similarly, a request can be made for certain types of music to be played, or for art work to be seen, and so on.

When the robotic aid responds, the human senses these changes and often utilize voices, physical motion or a display of imagery as control surfaces. The robotic aid would have corresponding sensors to translate the vocal, mechanical or pictorial commands. These are fused into appropriate electronic signals to be sent to the robot's computer.

The signals are processed within the robotic aid using typical AI algorithms.

AI algorithms include support vector machines, various types of neural networks, as well as clustering, regression algorithms and the like. The data processed is almost always adjusted by using information contained within an internal data base. This data base most often contains inputs from external data bases by way of transmission. A direct result, is a higher degree of learning and acquiring of human defined objectives. In any case, the output from the robotic aid consists of decisions that result in problem solving. Solutions might be the translation of language, the conversion of written words to audio, or the converse. As previously illustrated, solutions could involve changes to the environment including motion, thermal, visual, such as imagery and video, as well as odor effects.

Connections to external data bases are most prominent since this enables a gigantic amount of information to be made available. As previously mentioned, this information is gathered and stored in AI data farms. However, local memory usually contains numerous amounts of information. In particular, this data relies heavily upon questions and answers given to previous requests. However, local stored data is minute compared to that stored on data farms. Because more and more information is mined and subsequently stored on processors, more and more energy is needed for the data farms. The choice of using nuclear power instead of gas, oil, coal or hydro is the seed to the AI CANCER TIMEBOMB. *One should beware of the slightest amount of ionizing radiation.*

A2) Details of Transformer Neural Networks

A2.1) Embeddings

Within the transformer neural network model, word embedding networks are employed. They are used in calculating numerical tuple values for the embedding vectors. The process is first performed by pre-trained neural networks on gigantic amounts of data using back propagation algorithms, see (Giardina, 2024). With this approach, the embedding process could be regarded as a look up table technique. When an input word is encountered within the input sequence, it is compared to other words within the input string. The look up process is analogous to table look up. The initial examination is a search for the context. The context is identified and final vector representations are assigned to each word.

The gigantic AI data centers have thousands of processors. In these processors are stored words that have the same spelling, but might have different meanings. These words may also be pronounced differently. Such words are called homographs. It could be said that each such word has a distinct vector representation. Moreover, for each such word, other words with similar context have vector representations close to the specified word. These vectors are also stored and linked together.

An example of a homograph in which the spellings are identical, but the pronunciations are distinct, is given next. Such a word is minute, which can be a time unit. However, it can be used as a small amount. For instance in the warning: Beware of minute traces of ionizing radiation. In the latter case, the transformer mode has an advantage when voice is used as an input. The advantage is lost if only written inputs are allowed. The word minute is not a homonym since the pronunciation differs as well as its context.

Sometimes, homographs have several meanings, and again distinct pronunciations. For instance, 'lead' is the metal Pb, atomic number 82, and atomic mass 207. However, in the phrase: 'The AI CANCER TIMEBOMB will lead the way for ionizing radiation avoidance.' Here, the word 'lead' is used as indicating being first. Finally, 'lead' can also be a leash for an animal.

A2.2) Positional Encoding for the Transformer

The positional encoding layer of a transformer neural network keeps track where each word or token is located within the input string. The value must be unique and generalized to the size of the input sequence. In actual transform models a maximum size of 512 entries is chosen as the dimensional vector for positional encoding. Assuming that the input string of words is identified in numerical order: j = 1, 2, 3, 4, ... n, Then, even words within this input string are located at, 2, 4, 6,..., and they have values sin(j /$10000^{2k/n}$) for positional encoding. Similarly, for odd valued tokens, they are given by cos(j / $10000^{2k/n}$). Here, k is the tuple value within the vector representation.

An example will be helpful. However, for illustration purposes, a changes in the parameters will be made. In this case use for even words, sin(2jπ/$2^{2k/n}$). Next, for odd words use cos(2jπ/$2^{2k/n}$). Just like the original expressions, as the tuple number goes up, the frequency decreases within the sinusoidal.

Example A2.1)

Consider the n = four input words from the following phrase: 'Fission creates two entities'. For the first word, since it is at an odd location, we use cos($2j\pi/2^{k/2}$). Next, evaluating using j = 1, and then let k = 1, 2, 3, and then 4, provides a four tuple row vector: (cos($2\pi/2^{1/2}$) cos($2\pi/2$) cos($2\pi/2^{3/2}$) cos($2\pi/4$)). The vector can be evaluated, giving about, (.6 -1 -.5 0). This is the vector representation for the first word or token, involving fission. Similarly, the second word positional encoding can be found, it uses j = 2. Therefore, sin($2j\pi/2^{k/2}$) is employed. Upon substitution it gives another four tuple vector, (sin($4\pi/2^{1/2}$) sin($4\pi/2$) sin($4\pi/2^{3/2}$) sin($4\pi/4$)). As before it could be evaluated. Subsequently two other four tuple vectors must be found, by using, j = 3, and 4. Together the four distinct vectors provide the positional encoding.#

A2.3) Self-head Attention Module

In a self-head attention module, suppose that there are T words or tokens within the input string. Also, assume that the word embedding step has been performed, and that this is followed by positional encoding. Finally, let these two vectors be added together. This is the protocol. It results in a total of T token row vectors. Denote row vector i, by xi, where each vector has d tuples. In this module there are three matrices: query, Q; key, K; and value, V, are found using the previous layer in the encoder. See (Vaswani, 2017). The matrices are named in accordance with traditional search techniques. The query is the information sought. The key refers to the context; it is a more global indicator of the value and is not as specific as the value. The value consists of the actual information.

In the following, the mechanics are illustrated by assuming that these three matrices are known, and all are of dimension d by d. The next step is to form the query, key and value vectors. In this case, there are T of each, and all are one by d row vectors. Specifically: Query vectors qi = xi Q; Key vectors ki= xi K; Value vectors vi = xi V. The modified query matrix will have query vectors as rows. Therefore, it produces a T by d matrix, thus: q = (q1' q2' ... qT')', where the prime indicates matrix transpose. Similarly the T by d modified key matrix is given by k = (k1' k2' ... kT')', and the modified T by d value matrix is v = (v1' ... vT')'.

From these matrices a compatibility matrix can be found. It is given by C = q k'. Since, q is a T by d and k' is a d by T matrix, this results in a T by T matrix. This is the basic result. It has entries within the matrix that show how words within the input string are related to other words. In essence, entries within this matrix are inner products with other words.

Example A2.2)
Say that d = 2 and T = 3. If q1 = (.2 6), q2 = (1 .4), q3= (-1 4), k1 = (7 2),
k2 = (-4 2), k3 = (0 6.1). The associated modified query and key matrices are given by q and k, followed by C in respective order:

```
| .2   6 |   | 7   2.0 |   | 13.4   11.2   36.6 |
| 1   .4 |   | -4  2.0 |   | 7.8    -3.2   .24 0 |
| -1   4 |   | 0   6.1 |   | 1.0    12 .0  24.4 |.
```

In the matrix C the first row, third column number 36.6 is the largest. This number also arises in Figure A2.1), where the vector q_1, and k_3 are illustrated. They are very close, indeed the inner product shows this, by being very large, 36.6.

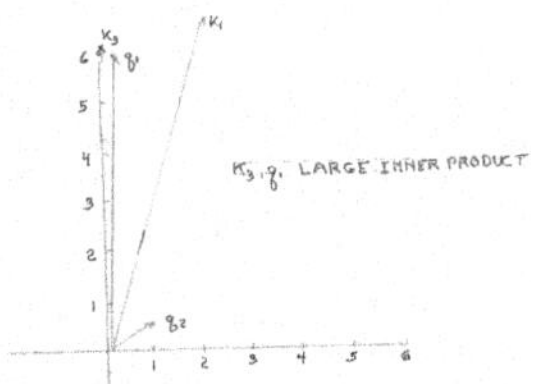

FIGURE A2.1) Large Inner Product

The next step in the process is to divide the C matrix by $d^{1/2}$. This makes the numbers smaller and easier for calculation. Thus $C^* = (q k')/ d^{1/2}$. The pseudo operation, Softmax is applied to each row of the C* matrix. Softmax is described in greater depth in (Giardina, 2024). In general, it is a heuristic and it is an arbitrary method for providing normalizing results. Indeed, for every entry within a fixed row of C*, replace entry c_k, by $e^{c_k}/\Sigma e^{c_j}$, where the sum goes from j = 1 to T.

As a consequence, entries of the resulting matrix are referred to as probabilities, and the matrix is called the attention matrix. It. Is denoted by A. Finally, the output of the attention block is R = A v, which is a T by d matrix.

A2.4) Multi-head Attention Module

For multi-head attention, the exact same method as the one described in the previous section is used. However, it can be performed h times with at most h = eight times in parallel. These matrices have reduced dimension, it is d/h. The method begins with computing h distinct query, key and value matrices. This means that h distinct, q, k and v matrices are constructed as before. Also, the R matrices should be calculated. These are dimension T by d/h and are called heads. The final attention matrix A is found by concatenating all these heads.

The matrix product is formed Q · K' = S. Here the prime denotes transpose and S is the score matrix. This operation is analogous to forming the inner product of each column vector within Q.

Entries within the S matrix shows the amount of emphasis words have on other words within the input. The larger the score the more dependency. It is followed by a normalization of S. Specifically, the calculation is to divide S by $d^{1/2}$, where d is the dimension of the Q and K matrices. This yields the normalized scaled matrix. Here, $S^* = S/d^{1/2}$. This step allows more stabled gradient calculations when the neural network is employed down the line. It helps lower chances of exploding gradients. Next, the pseudo operation, Softmax, is applied to the normalized score matrix. As before, the result of this operation is called the attention matrix A. The resulting matrix has entries between zero and one.

The numbers within A are interpreted to be probabilities, associating words from other words within the input string. The next calculation is to form $A \cdot V = Y$. The result, Y is called the output vector. It is inputted into a linear neural network which results in H, this is called an attention head. To obtain different heads containing different self attention mechanisms, the whole process is performed using different Q, K, and V matrices. This is performed up to the calculation of the output vector Y. In this case, the distinct output vectors are linked together in a sequence, called concatenation. Subsequently, value is input into the output module. And the process continues thusly.

A2.5) The Decoder Block

The decoder has sub-blocks similar to those in the encoder. One large difference is that the decoder cannot predict, it must be causal. In order to enforce causality, before the softmax pseudo operator is employed, a masking function is employed to the modified scaled score matrix S*. In this case, an entry by entry multiplication is performed to S* matrix, such that it becomes a lower triangle matrix with those entries invariant. While for entries column i greater than row j, values of minus infinity are applied. When the softmax operation is taken involving rows of the triangular matrix, the values with minus infinity values become zeros. Each entry within a row has values in the interval [0, 1]. Additionally, all entries within a row sum to one. The result is that probabilities are interpreted as entries within rows of the resulting triangular matrix.

A3) Survey of Nuclear Devices and Consequences

A brief description of nuclear applications are presented in an abbreviated time line. In 1939, the nuclear fission process was discovered. See Section 3.1, for an in-depth description of fission. The top secret atomic bomb, Trinity, used fission to cause the nuclear reaction in Los Alamos, New Mexico. The project was called the Manhattan Project, and took about two and a half years to complete. The fuel in this case, was Plutonium. The bomb was detonated in July 1945, a little south of Alba Queue, New Mexico. This would be the first nuclear bomb test among the 1,032 nuclear bombs tested by the US. The last test was performed, under ground in Nevada, 47 years after the Trinity test. (ATF, 2022).

The light from the Los Alamos mushroom cloud was seen in Mexico, in Arizona and Texas. White dust was dispersed over a large radius. Numerous people contacted cancer and subsequently died. Concurrently, the term Downwinder was coined. (CDC's LAHDRA, 2018). This term refers to humans exposed to ionizing radiation and nuclear end products due to wind directions. Further nuclear testing was conducted in New Mexico. Subsequently, RECA, the Radiation Exposure Compensation Act, was created in 1990 to provide renumeration to Downwinders. However, the Downwinders from New Mexico were denied compensation.

On August 6, 1945, the US bombed Hiroshima, Japan. It was an atom bomb as destructive as 28 thousand tons of TNT. The bomb was called Little Boy. This was followed by another bomb, called Fat Man. It landed three days later in Nagasaki, Japan. Within six days after the second bomb landing, Japan surrendered. In the following two years, many Japanese people developed leukemia. In following years many types of solid cancers also appeared. These are abnormal masses of tissue which are malignant. Among the solid cancers are sarcomas, lymphomas and carcinomas, but not leukemia.

Nine nuclear reactors, and five plutonium fabrication plants were built in the period, 1942-1943 in the city of Hanford, Washington. These structures are located in the southeastern part of the state,. Among the purposes for the reactors was the creation of isotopes to be used in nuclear bombs. The Columbia river was utilized to cool the graphite moderated, water cooled reactors. The reactors gave off a large amount of radiation contamination which was dumped into this river. To house this ionizing radiation, a hundred and seventy very large holding tanks were built to house the radioactive waste material. In the 1980's some sixty tanks were found to be leaking. These tanks had to be emptied. They were replaced with glass tanks constructed within a metal exterior. However, due to the large amounts of rain in the state of Washington, enormous amounts of radium and other isotopes leaked into the river. The state of Washington has the highest rate of cancer throughout the US, and Hanford remains the city with most IR.

During the period from Jan 27, 1951 to 1992 the US detonated about 928 large nuclear weapons in Nevada. One hundred were atmospheric, and 828 were underground. Many of these tests were conducted in Mercury, Nevada. (ATF, 2022). The mushroom cloud could be seen in several cities in Nevada, for instance, in Pahrump, Nevada where the Shoshone Indians live. There, many people developed cancer and died. This was due in part to the wind currents which carry radioactive fallout material throughout the US. The well known Area 51 is located in Nevada. Numerous workers and soldiers who were present in this area during the test periods are appealing for compensation due to IR causing cancer.

Most serious, heavy radioactive fallout of Iodine 131 occurred in St. George Utah. This isotope can enter the body through the consumption of contaminated food, drinks, or even by breathing contaminated air. Again, numerous people developed cancer, and these people are also called Downwinders. In particular, children developed leukemia at a rate three times higher than the national average. (DeGrraw, 2024). Subsequently, these Downwinders were compensated by RECA.

The motion picture, The Conqueror, was partially made in Snow Mountain, Utah in 1954. The crew consisted of about 220 people of which 120 died from cancer. They developed cancer within ten years after the filming. Many men in their thirties developed prostate cancer, and women caught thyroid cancer. The cause of cancer was linked to nuclear tests, conducted about 135 miles away in Mercury, Nevada. These tests were ten times more powerful than the bombs dropped on Japan. (DeGraw, 2024).

The first nuclear reactor for electricity generation occurred in Idaho Falls Idaho. A town of nineteen thousand people at the time. In January 1949, the Idaho Falls site was considered for the creation of a new nuclear reactors among five other sites, including one in Montana. A 170,000 acre ARCO Proving Grounds was nearby, run by the US Navy. Later in 1949 Idaho Falls was chosen. It also acquired the Navy proving grounds, along with an additional 230,000 acres surrounding the proving grounds. In 1951, the Experimental Breeder Reactor EBR, was shown to generate increasingly large amounts of electricity. At success lead to the creation of NRTS, the National Reactor Testing Station. (Hampshire, 2023).

In 1951, Admiral Hyman Rickover proposed the construction of a nuclear powered submarine. (Nuclear Museum, 2022). Later that year, congress gave its approval. Contracts went out to GE to create a liquid metal cooled reactor using sodium. Simultaneously, the Westinghouse Company was commissioned to build a Pressurized Water Reactor, PWR. The latter reactor was mentioned in Section 3.2. It has two separate water channels, which were not connected. The first cools the uranium fuel and is pressurized so as not to produce steam. The second obtains heat from the first channel by a heat transfer protocol. The second channel then produces steam for the turbine. In 1953, this reactor went critical, that is it had enough material to continue the fission process. In 1955, this type of reactor successfully powered the first nuclear submarine, the Nautilus.

Later GE used a sodium cooled reactor to power the submarine Seawolf. Due to the harmful reactions of sodium with water, an immediate abandonment of the project was ordered. In turn, GE began using , Boiling Water Reactors, BWR, see Section 3.2, where an illustration is provided.

The first general purpose large scale nuclear PWR plant was built by Westinghouse in 1958. This was called, Shippingport Atomic Power Station, located in Shippingport Pa. For more details see, (NuclearNewswire, 2017).

The Kyshtym disaster is often said to be the fourth most destructive nuclear accident. It started when a tank containing fuel consisting of fission nuclides exploded in the Mayak Nuclear Reacting Plant in 1957. These waste tanks are located near Chelyabinsk, Russia. More than 200 people died immediately from the explosion. Additionally, thousands of people and animals were showered with radioactive particles. In Mayak, a city nearby, the radioactive waste material was dumped in

Karachai Lake. However, the lake is connected to the Techa River in Russia. This river carried IR for far distances, and flooded nearby villages. The river contained radiation much higher than sufficient to kill a person in a short amount of time.

People were evacuated and given about thirty thousand dollars for doing so. However, those who stayed were often contaminated and developed cancer. A major contribution to cancer and death was due to radioactivity which contaminated the milk and water. Along with this, eating fish from the Techa River was to blame, since contamination of Plutonium 239, and 240 existed in the river. Studies of people who lived in known contaminated areas showed that they were not aware of the danger due to IR. Most dangerous, Kryptom 85 was observed; it poured out of nuclear reactor smoke stacks. The isotope is created during fission involving uranium and plutonium. This gas has a little more than a ten year half life. The smaller the half life, the more dangerous the substance. On the other hand, the larger the half life, the longer it will last. This enables longer durations of time for food, water and animals to be exposed to this substance. The isotope Kryptom 85 is well known to cause various cancers. However, a different isotope, Krypton 83 is used in MRI, Magnetic Resonance Imaging.

A partial meltdown occurred in 1959 at the Santa Susana Field Testing, SSFT in California. There were ten nuclear reactors at SSFT. Specifically, the disaster occurred in a nuclear reactor SRE, which was used to sell electricity to the public in Moore Park. There was no containment building for the liquid sodium graphite moderated reactor. A single loop of liquid sodium is used to cool the radioactive source. This substance is mixed with nuclear elements within the reactor. Additionally, it is employed utilizing heat exchange methods, where it heats another loop of liquid. This isolated second loop was used for running the turbines, thereby generating electricity. A revealing report on this disaster is provided in, (Engineering.com, 2020).

A pressure excursion occurred at SSFT in 1959. Because of the undesired power surge a large number of emergency shut downs were performed. These were due to various effects such as failed switches, trapped liquid cells, as well as an explosion due to non careful containment procedures. Erratic temperatures, as well as various reactor elements being stuck were again experienced. It was also noticed that various stainless steel enclosures had missing clad. Sodium oxide was found, but the amount of radiation released was not acknowledged.

At that time they did not look for Cesium 137, Cs 137 or Iodine 131, I 131.

Subsequently, it was claimed that this release of ionizing radiation at SSFT was 260 times that which was released from the Three Mile Island disaster. The Three Mile Island incident occurred some twenty years later. This disclosure was provided in 1979, and described by J. Blumenfeld, head of the California Environmental Protection Area. He said that it resulted in one of the most toxic sites in the US. As time went on almost a million people moved in the vicinity. Many builders of homes did not explain or mention the existence of SSFT to many home buyers.

A report was documented on the SSFT disaster by the SSFT advisory panel. It provided independent scientific studies of potential community impacts from the SSFT meltdown, as well as other contaminations released by accidents at that time. Also, the October 2006 Report of the SSFT advisory panel stated that 260 cancer deaths were related to these accidents. Numerous contaminants of concern included Cesium 137, Strontium 90, Plutonium 239, as well as Tritium. Sampling in some places showed one thousand times the background radionuclides at SSFT than elsewhere. In 2016, a

Boeing report said that if one hundred people lived on a specific site of SSFT, then 96 would soon get cancer. After, Boeing proposed a cleanup of the region. The cleanup affected a reduction in these numbers. So that only 5 to 10 people, among 100 would soon acquire cancer.

H. Morgenstern, an Epyologist, at U of Michigan, provided a study, showing that from 1995 to 1998, the incidence rate of cancer was 60% greater among residents living within two miles than among residents living more than five miles, from SSFT. This holds for solid cancers like thyroid, oral, and nasal cavities, pharynx larynx esophagus, bladder, lymph's and myelomas. The result also holds for blood cancers.

The first US nuclear disaster reporting the killing of several people occurred January 3, 1961. This was at a small nuclear reactor testing station at the Army nuclear research center in Idaho. This center was controlled by three men. (O'Conner, 2007). After numerous fire alarms going off, fire fighters were sent to the site. Upon arriving they found that there had been a meltdown and there exists very high radiation levels. Inspecting the premises, two crewman's bodies were found, one had already died. However, so did the other one, on the way to the hospital. The third body was found pinned on the roof of the building. He was pierced thru the body with a control rod attached to the ceiling.

It was conjectured that the person whose body was pinned to the ceiling, had moved a control rod too far out from the reactor. This caused a bomb type explosion. It was later claimed that the control rod got stuck, and yanked out too far. From the explosion, about thirty percent of the fuel disappeared. As a result of this disaster, new reliability requirements for nuclear reactors were created. For instance, all current reactors should never have a single point fault.

In 1963 The USS Thresher nuclear submarine sank, killing 129 crew members aboard. It was the first nuclear attack submarine. Originally, it was thought that a pressured pipe bursted causing flooding. SCRAM was enforced to shut down the nuclear reactor. SCRAM is emergency shut down of a nuclear reactor. Electric propulsion could not take over. Later it was assumed that electrical problems, as well as piping joint problems existed, again causing SCRAM. The submarine could go 1/4 mile below surface safely. However, it was found, fragmented in pieces, within a year later, 8,400 feet below sea level. (News Release, 1964). The exact cause of the disaster is not known.

Early on, almost all countries disposed of radioactive material in the bottom of the ocean. A hundred tons of nuclear waste was dumped, and about eighty percent was dumped by England. In 1993, using the ocean to dump radioactive waste was forbidden.

France, England and Japan recycle the spent fuel. But only about 10% is actually recycled. Spent fuel pools are noted to be dangerous. This is due to planes flying over and targeting these sites with bombs. Additionally, there is the fear that terrorists might disrupt these pools. In France, radioactive waste is stored very far underground in layers of clay. These substances are stored in glass encasements with stainless steel containments. Eventually, the radioactive substance will corrode the encasement, and in many, many years, perhaps two hundred thousand years. radioactive material will rise thru the clay.

In 1979, The Three Mile Island, PWR disaster occurred. The feed water pump in reactor two failed. Maintenance of these plants was under par. High levels of radiation were recorded. The radiation above the containment building effectively read,

800rem/hour. This is the maximum dose a human can tolerate in a half a second before death arises. Radioactive cooling water was discharged before overflowing. Radioactive gasses were let out into the environment from this disaster. These were isotopes of Krypton 85 and Xenon 133. Above the smoke stacks a recording of 1200 mrems/hr was documented consisting of these two isotopes. Krypton 85 was described previously. Similarly, Xenon 133 has a half life of about ten years. Xenon 133 employed in medical imaging, involving the brain, liver and blood. It is one of the rarest gasses.

As well as great economic loss, numerous people alleged health defects due to The Three Mile Island disaster. An appeal was made for monetary help, however, the US District Court Judge presiding over the matter dismissed the entire case. Interesting reading and suggestions can be found in, ((NIH) (.gov), 1986).

In short, due to the introduction of fission and fusion, there are very large amounts of nuclear waste and ionizing radiation in the environment. It exists from past bomb tests, as well as from nuclear reactor discarded materials and failures. The necessary, and current, use of nuclear for defense, research and medical is more than enough. There is no need to employ additional nuclear for generating energy for AI purposes. *The slightest amount of additional radiation would be harmful.*

The worst nuclear reactor disaster was reported to be Chernobyl, in the Ukraine 1986. At that time there were four reactors, and six more were to be built. They were being constructed to enable Chernobyl to become the center for Russia's nuclear power. The disaster happened during a safety shut down test. (World Nuclear Association, 2024). The SCRAM device that shuts down the reactor in case of emergencies was disabled before the test. The main cause for the disaster is a large design flaw. It is unclear, but the design flaw was speculated to be known, at least to the upper commands. However, it was not known to the workers at the site. It seems that pressure in the fuel assembly produced a surge in power. This resulted in several control rods needed to reduce the fission process getting stuck. The overpressure caused the reactor to become a bomb. This resulted in an exposed core, due to a one thousand ton cover plate being ruptured.

It is reported that a larger second explosion occurred. It reportedly produced radioactive graphite to be tossed for large distances along with ionizing radiation. The graphite in this type of BWR is used as a moderator. This radiation was experienced throughout Europe. A day and a half later, evacuation of the residents of the city of Prypiat and its surrounds were carried out. Some 350,000 people left, and almost 2,000 remained. Near the plant, the radiation was measured to be 2000mr/h. In the town, it was between 60mr/h and 200mr/hr. Twenty thousand tons of radiated water had to be drained. Some 237 people had acute radiation sickness, 37 died within a month or so. Cancer related deaths are estimated to be 4,000. Children present at the time had a 90% chance of getting cancer.

The Fukushima disaster in 2011 had at least one good result. It halted US creation of any new nuclear reactors for the next 13 years. The Fukushima disaster involved a BWR which was built by GE. The disaster occurred due to a magnitude 9 earthquake, which was followed by a tsunami. The earthquake and tsunami caused backup generators for the reactors to be damaged. The three reactors were said to be shut off, but the excessive heat caused fuel rods to melt down. This material fell into containment vessels, and exposed the core. Subsequently, numerous explosions occurred days apart. A direct result was that about 20,000 people died immediately. Almost one hundred and fifty thousand of people were evacuated.

The contamination from the Fukushima disaster is expected to be removed in about 50 years, and robots are being employed in the endeavor. People who lived in the vicinity of the disaster were exposed to radiation in the air and on the ground. Among the radionuclides released were Iodine 131, I 131, and Cesium 137, Cs 137. The latter has a half life of eight days, making it most dangerous. It can cause cancer by inhaling as well as eating or drinking contaminated foods or liquids. Iodine 131 was previously described when referring to the most environmental unfriendly city in the US, Hanover, Washington. Additionally, it is referred to in the SSFL disaster.

The 2018 Woolsey fire, which initially covered 300 acres started at the Chatsworth Sub station, a position where the nuclear meltdown occurred years earlier. This station is located in the SSFT. Eventually, the fire grew to 1,000 acres. The dust and ashes contained some radioactive particles scattered from the fire. The most critical time for ionizing radiation exposure is when these ashes fall. Examination of the ashes showed, a large contradiction with the California government's analysis. There are actually high levels of radioactive particles which had fell in neighborhoods due to this fire. (Kaltofeen, et al, 2021). (Engineering.com, 2020). Additionally, a 2012 EPA report stated that one out of every seven soil samples in SSFT contained radioactive materials beyond safe limits.

More than eighty years of ionizing radiation, and ineptly stored nuclear waste material, has polluted our country. Employing nuclear energy for AI farms is a Ticking TIMEBOMB. Follow President Trump's lead - gas, coal, oil and hydro power is a safer path to avoid the AI CANCER TIMEBOMB.

References

ATF, Atomic Heritage Foundation, Nevada test site, 2022.

Averbeck, A., and Rodriguer-Lafrasse, C., Role of mitochondria in radiation responses: epigenetic, metabolic, and signaling impacts, International Journal of Molecular Sciences, 2020.

B D Editors, RNA Polymerase, Biology Dictionary, 2019.

CDC,LAHDRA, Los Alamos Historical Document Retrieval and Assessment, Final Report, 2018.

Coursera staff, The history of AI: A timeline of AI, Coursera 2024.

DeGraw, S., Nuclear fallout: documentary unveiling tragic legacy of “The Conquerer” to screen in St. George, St George News, 2024.

Dougherty, E., and Giardina, C., Mathematical Methods for Artificial Intelligence and Automatous Systems, Prentice Hall, 1988.

Duraj, T., et al, Clinical research framework proposal for ketogenic metabolic therapy in glioblastoma, BMC Medicine 2024.

Electrak, Amazon just bought a 100% nuclear powered data center, 2024.

Engineering.com, America's worst nuclear disaster was in California, who knew?, Engineering.com, 2020.

Giardina, C., Many-Sorted Algebras for Deep Learning and Quantum Technology. Elsevier, 2024.

Giardina, C., Probability for Deep Learning Quantum, A Many-Sorted Algebra View, Elsevier, 2025.

Hampshire, J., The legacy of the National Reactor Testing Station, today's Idaho National Laboratory, Studsvik, 2023.

Helmenstine, A., Mitochondria - definition, structure, function, Science Notes, 2024.

Huang, M., et al, Targeting glutamine metabolism to enhance immunoprevention of EGFR-Driven lung cancer, Advanced Science 9 (26), 2022.

Kaltofeen, M., et al, Radioactive micro particles related to the Woolsey fire in Simi Valley, Ca, Science Direct, Elsevier, 2021.

Kraft, and Lockner, Mitochondrial anchors: positioning mitochondria and more, Elsevier, 2018.

Lazaro, E., Scientists find cell-free mitochondria in human blood, Sci News, 2025.

Leija, R., et al, The mitochondrial lactate oxidation complex: endpoint for carbohydrate carbon disposal, Research Article, American Physiological Society, 2017.

Lenzen, S., A fresh view of glycolysis and glucokinase regulation, J Biol Chem, 2014.

Lloyd, C., et al, The effects of U232 on enrichment and. Material attractiveness over time, Science Direct, Elsevier, 2019.

Mazur Instruments, User manual, PRM nuclear radiation manual, 2017.

NIH (.gov), Three Mile Island and Bhopal: lessons learned and not learned, National Library of Medicine,1986.

Mills,A., Use of hyperbaric oxygen as an adjunct in the treatment of radio necrosis, ETDEWEB, Dept. Energy, 1978

Moore, and Stanitiski, 2014), Chemistry the molecular science, Cengage Learning, 2014.

NIH (.gov), Three Mile Island and Bhopal: lessons learned and not learned, National Library of Medicine,1986.

NEI.org, Used fuel storage and nuclear waste fund payments by states, 2022.

News Release, Office of Assistant Secretary of Defense (Public Affair), Wash. D C, Oct. 1, 1964.

NRC.gov, Measuring radiation, 2020.

NRC.gov, Biological effects of radiation, Reactor Concept Manual, 2014.

Nuclear Museum, Hyman G. Rickover, Atomic Heritage Foundation, 2022.

NuclearNewswire, Shippingport atomic power station: five fast facts, American Nuclear Society, 2017.

O'Conner, B., Supercritical: SI-1 Nuclear reactor explosion, NASA, 2007

Patel, S., How Westinghouse symbol of US nuclear power, collapsed. POWER, IEU, 2017.

Rao, S., Mitochondrial changes in cancer, National Library of Medicine, 2016.

Rong, Z., et al, The mitochondrial response to DNA damage, Frontiers in Cell and Development Biology, 2021.

RREM, Radiation units and conversion factors - HHS.gov, Radiation Emergency Medical Management, 2025.

Sayegh, E., The billion dollar AI gamble: data centers the new high stakes game, Forbes, 2024.

Seyfried, T., Cancer as a mitochondrial metabolic disease, Frontiers in Cell and Developmental Biology, 2015.

Seyfried, T., et al Considerations of ketogenic metabolic therapy as a complementary or alternative approach for managing breast cancer, Frontiers in Nutrition, 2020.

Su, E., et al, Mitochondria: at the crossroads between mechanobiology and cell metabolism, Pub Med, 2023.

Sutskever, N., et al, Sequence to sequence learning with NN, Google, 2014.

Tatomir, J., DNA and RNA Mutations Study.com. 2024.

Trump, D., AI for the American people, Executive Order, US Gov. 2019.

U.S.NRC, Calculator to measure annual dose of radiation, 2021.

Vaswani, A., et al, Attention is all you need, Google Brain, 2017.

Vincent, A., Mitochondrial nanotunnels, Trends in Biology, 2017.

Wang, B., et al, A glutamine tug-of-war between cancer and immune cells: recent advances in unraveling the ongoing battle, Journal of Experimental & Clinical Cancer Research, 2024.

Warburg, O., On the origin of cancer cells, Science, 24 Feb 1956. (Rao, 2016).

World Nuclear Association, Chernobyl Accident 1986, 2024.

About the Author

Dr. Giardina was a professor of mathematics, electrical engineering, and computer science at Fairleigh Dickinson University from 1965 to 1982. From 1982 to 1986, he was a professor at the Stevens Institute of Technology. On behalf of these two universities he headed off campus programs at various industrial and military locations, such as Fort Monmouth, ITT, Bendix, Bell Labs, Bellcore, and Kearfott, all in NJ.From 1986 to 1999, he was a professor at the College of Staten Island, City University of New York.

His industrial career began at Transil Semiconductors, Englewood NJ in 1963. Subsequently he was awarded a Communication Development Training fellowship at Bell Telephone Laboratories, Whippany, NJ, United States where he worked in military defense. He continued in the area of military defense and research in 1968 at Singer Kearfott, Wayne NJ. Later in 1996, he again joined Bell Telephone Laboratories, Whippany, NJ, United States.

Finally, in 1998, Dr. Giardina returned to Kearfott, then called BAE Systems as a Senior Member of the Technical Staff.

His research interests include digital signal and image processing, pattern recognition, artificial intelligence, and the constructive theory of functions. Dr. Giardina has authored numerous papers and several books in these areas, including: Mathematical Models for Artificial Intelligence and Autonomous Systems; Matrix Structure Image Processing; Morphological Methods in Image and Signal Processing; Image Processing—Continuous to Discrete; all with Prentice Hall; Parallel Digital Signal Processing: A Unified Signal Algebra Approach, Regency; and A Unified Signal Algebra Approach to Two-Dimensional Parallel Digital Signal Processing, Chapman and Hall/CRC Press. Most recently he authored: Many-Sorted Algebras for Deep Learning and Quantum Technology, Feb 2024; Probability for Deep Learning Quantum, A Many-Sorted Algebra View, Jan 2025, both Elsevier.

Dedication

To My Betty, My Everything.

Acknowledgements

Thanks goes to Ed Cooke for reading the manuscript and making excellent corrections. After numerous attempts for a title, Ed proposed the AI CANCER TIMEBOMB, A most appropriate and timely description for the work.

Thanks also, to Brian Moseley, form the Apple Store in San Luis Obispo. Without his help, page numbers would not be page numbers!

Special thanks to Bob Hudson for the great improvements he made in just about all my arguments. While not changing the meaning of concepts, he transformed Bronx language into English.

www.ingramcontent.com/pod-product-compliance
Lightning Source LLC
LaVergne TN
LVHW022053200926
848481LV00003B/894